TARGET FILTON

TARGET FILTON

*The two Luftwaffe attacks
in September 1940*

KENNETH WAKEFIELD

With an introduction by
Generalmajor a. D. Friedrich Kless

REDCLIFFE
Bristol

First published in 1979 by
William Kimber & Co.Ltd.

This edition first published in 1990
by Redcliffe Press Ltd.,
49 Park St., Bristol

© Kenneth Wakefield

ISBN 1 872971 55 5

Printed by
WBC Print Ltd., Bridgend

Contents

		Page
	Introduction	
	by Generalmajor a.D. Friedrich Kless	11
	Prologue	13
	Acknowledgements	15
	Bibliographical note	17
	Glossary of German terms	21
I	Target: Filton	25
II	For and Against	37
III	To the Normandy Coast	52
IV	Confusion in Defence	71
V	Bomben Los!	81
VI	War over Wessex	94
VII	The Stricken Factory	107
VIII	Unwelcome Guests – 1	114
IX	Unwelcome Guests – 2	123
X	Claim and Counterclaim	142
XI	A Timely Move	148
XII	Rout in the Sun	164
XIII	Destroyers Destroyed	183
XIV	Postscript	194

Appendix:

1	Organisation and Senior Officers of KG 55	200
2	Order of Battle, No 10 Group Fighter Command	201
3	British Participants in the Defence of Filton	202
4	RAF Combat Claims in the Defence of Filton	203
5	RAF Casualties in the Defence of Filton	204
6	German Casualties in the Attack on Filton	205
7	British Participants in the Defence of Yate	207
8	RAF Combat claims in the Defence of Yate	209

 9 RAF Casualties in the Defence of Yate   209
10 German Casualties in the Attack on Yate   210
11 Aircraft Specifications and Performance   212
Index   217

List of Illustrations

                                                              Page
Major Friedrich Kless. (*F. Kless*)   10
Filton Aerodrome, 1931. (*Flight International*)   27
Blenheim Mk IVs in production at Filton. (*British Aerospace*) 29
Blenheim Roll-out. (*British Aerospace*)   29
Bristol Perseus engines in production at Patchway.
                                       (*British Aerospace*)   30
Target photograph of Filton, September 1940.   31
Target map of Filton.   33
Target map of Filton Airfield.   35
Defenders of Bristol.   41
No 10 Group Operations Room. (*Imperial War Museum*)   42
Göring visits KG 55, 1939. (*M. Reiser*)   45
The Operations HQ of III Gruppe, KG 55. (*M. Reiser*)   46
He 111P2 of 9/KG 55. (*Bundesarchiv*)   47
Oberstleutnant Joachim-Friedrich Huth.   49
Hauptmann Wilhelm Makrocki.   49
Hauptmann Hans Schalk.   49
Hauptmann Ralph von Rettburg.   49
Bf 110 C4s of 3/ZG 26. (*J. Koepsell*)   50
Bf 109 E of the Guernsey-based 4/JG 53. (*M. Payne*)   51
Karl Gerdsmeier. (*K. Gerdsmeier*)   54
Gerdsmeier in his He 111. (*K. Gerdsmeier*)   54
Karl Gerdsmeier's He 111. (*K. Gerdsmeier*)   60
Oberleutnant Weigel's He 111. (*K. Gerdsmeier*)   61
Feldwebel Martin Reiser. (*M. Reiser*)   62
Leutnant Tüffers. (*M. Reiser*)   63
Preparing for Take off. (*M. Reiser*)   64
Boarding an He 111 at Villacoublay. (*M. Reiser*)   64
Werner Oberländer. (*W. Oberländer*)   66
He 111Ps of 9/KG 55, Villacoublay. (*W. Oberländer*)   67

Pilot Officer Eric S. Marrs.   78
Gunners of 237 Battery, 76th HAA Regiment, RA.
                                              (*K. Grater*)   85
"An Attack and its Results." (*Der Adler*)   91
Feldwebel Walter Scherer. (*Grete Scherer*)   98
The last moments of Hans Bröcker's He 111.   100
The crash of G1+LR at Poole.   101
Villacoublay. (*M. Reiser*)   104
Roll of Honour. (*British Aerospace*)   106
Reconnaissance photo of Filton, 27th September 1940.
                                              (*A. Herbst*) 110
Beaufighter Mk I night fighter at Filton. (*British Aerospace*) 111
The final assembly plate of G1+DN.   122
Walter Scherer's Bf 110 C4. (*Grete Scherer*)   125
Walter Scherer in Düsseldorf. (*Grete Scherer*)   126
Unteroffizier Kurt Schraps. (*K. Schraps*)   129
Kurt Schraps parachuting into the sea.   130
Unteroffizier Günter Weidner (*K. Schraps*)   132
Unteroffizier Kurt Schraps. (*K. Schraps*)   132
G1+BH crash-landed at Studland.   135
Hauptman Karl Köthke. (*K. Köthke*)   137
Studland crash survivors. (*K. Köthke*)   139
A Messerschmitt AG advertisement.   150
Flight Lieutenant W. Barrington Royce. (*W.B. Royce*)   152
Pilot Officer Murray Frisby. (*W.B. Royce*)   152
Squadron Leader John Sample. (*W.B. Royce*)   155
Hauptmann Martin Lutz.   157
Parnall Aircraft, Yate. (*Parnall Aircraft*)   159
Target map of Yate.   161
Target map of Yate.   163
Hurricanes of 56 Squadron. (*Imperial War Museum*)   166
Flight Lieutenant W. Barrington Royce. (*W.B. Royce*)   167
504 Squadron pilots at Readiness. (*W.B. Royce*)   168
Pilot Officer Murray Frisby. (*W.B. Royce*)   169
Messerschmitt Bf 110 C4 (U8+FK). (*via Peter Cornwell*)   170
Oxygen bottles and fuselage wreckage of the Bf 110 shot
   down at Fishponds.   (*Imperial War Museum*)   172
Bf 110 crash at Fishponds, Bristol. (*Bristol Evening Post*) 174

Filton Crew Hut. (*W.B. Royce*)   175
Leutnant Joachim Koepsell. (*J. Koepsell*)   177
Johann Schmidt in the rear cockpit. (*J. Koepsell*)   181
A portion of the starboard fin of Bf 110 U8+CL.   181
NCOs of 504 Squadron at Filton, 1940. (*W.B. Royce*)   185
Hurricane TM:Q at Filton, 1940. (*W.B. Royce*)   185
Oberleutnant Wilhelm Rössiger.   192
Supermarine Spitfire Mk IA R6915. (*Imperial War Museum*)   197

MAPS

The Defence of the West Country   39
Places mentioned in operations   70
The Attack on Filton   73

Uncredited photographs are via
the Kenneth Wakefield Collection.

Attack Leader. Major Friedrich Kless, the Gruppenkommandeur of II/KG 55 and leader of the attack on Filton, 25th September 1940.

Introduction

by Generalmajor a.D. Friedrich Kless
German Air Force

From the culminating point of the Battle of Britain my friend Ken Wakefield has selected two episodes which he considers to be characteristic and has described them in great detail with admirable care, clarity and objectivity.

As the officer commanding the German bombing attack against the Filton aero-engine works at Bristol on 25th September 1940, I can vouch for the correctness of the description of events so far as the German side is concerned.

Sincere thanks and high recognition are due to the author for his objective narration. Each line bears witness to his endeavour to do justice to both sides, to reject the propaganda elements of those days and to correct erroneous statements which, in the heat of battle at the time, were inevitable.

More than a generation has passed since the historic events of those trying years. The long sequence of vicissitudes that followed the Battle of Britain – and particularly the struggle with the Soviet Union – have naturally become superimposed on my memory and the memories of my few surviving comrades. But the Battle of Britain had been ingrained in the minds of German fighter and bomber crews because, in contrast with other campaigns, that particular struggle was exclusively one between flying units.

Like our British comrades we felt the historical significance of those events. Both sides were spurred to the utmost and made, and caused, sacrifices in a measure hardly ever before levied against each other by two nations.

The German bomber group (Kampfgeschwader 55) to which I belonged had a scheduled strength of one hundred crews of five men each. During the total course of the war 710 airmen belonging to it were killed in action, 747 went missing, and 174 were taken prisoner-of-war after being shot down; the group lost its scheduled number of crews thrice over. The survivors fought on to the end.

Conditions on the British side may well have been as sacrificial. Every élite has to pay its due to destiny.

We operational crews of the war generation experienced the full brunt of the harshness of fighting the Royal Air Force. We always recognised, indeed appreciated, the flying skills and fighting spirit of the British fighters, driving courageous wedges into our formations with enormous valour. We were full of respect for them and indeed we often felt proud to fight so worthy a foe, even when so doing we lost many comrades and brothers. Certainly in the sworn band of brothers ready to risk their lives daily we included those fighting against us.

Subsequent generations may find in the memories of sacrifice and comradeship experienced by both sides heartening tokens of genuine and eternal value, combined with examples of courage in the most demanding circumstances.

Apart from the desert campaigns of North Africa, the Battle of Britain appears to have been the last great chivalrous struggle. Fairness and chivalry did indeed mark our attitudes and efforts, as did military loyalty and obedience. But we also certainly felt that these were the dying throes of chivalrous warfare; we keenly felt the spiritual rifts, the end of an era. Already by then the thoughtful few were almost overwhelmed by the fratricide of the Western Hemisphere, the mutual annihilation.

The young generations of today are in the fortunate position of being able to turn to better, more human ideals. May they draw the conclusion from this book that the countries of Europe's core are capable of great achievements if only they unite their efforts instead of turning against each other.

The old respect for one another – and the new trust in each other – might well help the younger generations see the virtue in the memories of their fathers and grandfathers, and achieve with vigour the happy consequences that they deserve.

Friedrich Kless.

Prologue

Most British people see the Battle of Britain as a German air offensive that ended in October 1940 with a resounding victory for the Royal Air Force, a victory that directly prevented the invasion of their homeland. In Germany the battle is more usually seen as an inconclusive struggle that did not peter out until June 1941 when Hitler turned his attention to Soviet Russia. Somewhere between the two viewpoints probably lies the truth – a narrow defeat of the Luftwaffe, aided by the onset of winter and, later on, by a German preoccupation with the forthcoming offensive in the East.

Both sides agree, however, that the fortunes of the German Air Force greatly fluctuated, and this was never more apparent than during the later stages of the great daylight raids over England in the autumn of 1940. Numerous examples can be found to illustrate the degrees of success and failure experienced almost in unison at this time, but possibly none highlights this strange disparity better than the two chosen for detailed analysis in this book. Yet, seemingly odd to relate, they occurred within the space of about forty-eight hours and took place over the same area.

The attacks are of interest for other reasons, not the least being that one of them reveals one of the rare occasions when RAF Fighter Command was found wanting. While in no way detracting from the skill and bravery of the German airmen involved, it is true to say that the first attack succeeded largely because on the day in question the British fighter control system was not at its best. The encore of two days later nearly succeeded, too, but good anticipation in a tactical organisation sense saved the day.

Also of interest is the fact that the operations here examined in detail took place outside the region more usually associated with the Battle, but by no means did all the action of that struggle occur over South-East England, as is popularly imagined. There is, too, some controversy over certain aspects of these attacks and it is hoped that this account will resolve most if not all the arguments, myths and wartime propaganda inspired half-truths that surround them and which have persisted over the years. But perhaps above all, for the student of air operations in World War Two, this reconstruction of the events of two days in September 1940 provides a detailed insight into the planning and execution of German bomber and fighter-bomber operations and the tactics employed by both sides during a vital phase of the Battle of Britain.

Acknowledgments

While this book is largely based on information gleaned from British and German official records, considerable use has been made of personal recollections supported by private documents including diaries, flying log books, and the like. Thus, in addition to my grateful thanks to Herr Noack of the Bundesarchiv, Herr Wank of the Deutsche Dienststelle, the Air Historical Branch of the Ministry of Defence and the Public Records Office, my thanks for their generous help go to a large number of people. In particular I would like to mention Friedrich Kless, Karl Gerdsmeier, Martin Reiser, Werner Oberländer, Georg Engel, Karl Köthke, Frau Grete Scherer, Fritz Jürges, Karl Geib, Kurt Schraps, Rudolf Weisbach and Joachim Koepsell, all from 'the other side of the fence', while in Britain my grateful appreciation goes to W. Barrington Royce, Douglas Wingrove, Kenneth Grater, Mrs Annie Tranter, Thomas Meadway, 'Chubby' Ball, Leslie Barnes, Miss Dorothy Cooke, the late Dr G.A. Valentine, A.H. Richards, Mr and Mrs Leslie Matthews, John Taylor, L.W. Trew, Theo Janku, J.P.H. Warner, Mr and Mrs Marshallsay, the late Ralph Wightman, and Wilfred Candy. Many others, too numerous to list, also delved back into the past and to them I am also grateful; it is quite impossible to mention everyone, as I am sure they will understand. Mention must be made, however, of Steve Ashcroft and Mervyn Amundson who gave so much help with the production of photographs and other material.

Many of the photographs used in this book originated from the people acknowledged above; others appear by kind permission of the Imperial War Museum, the Bundesarchiv, British Aerospace, Michael Payne, Peter Cornwell and the Editors of *Flight International* and the *Bristol Evening Post*. To the latter I also extend my thanks for permission to quote certain reports and comments.

Finally, but perhaps most important of all, my thanks and sincere appreciation go to my brother-in-law and co-researcher, Cliff Vincent. Without his unstinting help and encouragement this book would never have materialised.

Bibliographical Note

In an attempt to maintain continuity in the main text of this book I have deliberately refrained from the extensive use of footnotes to indicate sources. It is necessary, therefore, to indicate in this short bibliographical note the kind of documentary evidence upon which it is based.

Rather than lean on previously published accounts of the Battle of Britain, extensive use has been made of primary sources. These include Royal Air Force and Air Ministry documents, held in the Public Record Office and in the Air Historical Branch of the Ministry of Defence, and German records maintained by the Bundesarchiv-Militärarchiv. British records consulted were Command, Group, Station and Squadron Operations Record Books, Combat Reports, Combat and Casualty Reports, and Air Ministry and Fighter Command Intelligence Summaries. Numerous other reports, correspondence files, minutes and other documents now in the Public Records Office were also examined.

Compared with British records the German material for the period is much less extensive, as one might expect, but sufficient documents have survived to permit a detailed reconstruction of Luftwaffe operations over Britain in 1940. These include daily situation reports, operations summaries and maps, and casualty (aircraft and personnel) lists. Detailed information concerning wartime flying personnel is retained by the Deutsche Dienststelle, while privately held documents, such as personal flying log books, also revealed much that is relevant.

In addition to British and German air force documents I have made use of various Civil Defence records including Ministry of

Home Security Operations Bulletins and Civil Defence (South-West Region) Daily Summaries. Information was also obtained from many private letters, papers, notebooks and diaries of the time, proffered by people willing and anxious to help in the compilation of an authentic account of the happenings of nearly forty years ago.

Previously published books on the Battle of Britain differ in their portrayal of certain events including, invariably, the operations described in this book. With the documentary evidence now available it is clear that some of these earlier books are of doubtful historical value and rare indeed is the book that is totally free of error. Some published shortly after the events that they describe, are slanted in a nationalistic manner and are somewhat polluted by propaganda. But that is understandable and they are nevertheless invaluable in recreating the atmosphere of 1940 and reveal how situations appeared at the time.

For those seeking a comprehensive list of books on the subject I would recommend the bibliography of Richard Collier's *Eagle Day* (Hodder and Stoughton, Ltd., London, 1966). The majority have something worthwhile to offer, but none more than Basil Collier's magnificent *The Defence of The United Kingdom* in the official *History of The Second World War* Series (HMSO, London, 1957). Praiseworthy, too, is *The Narrow Margin*, the work of Derek Wood and Derek Dempster (Hutchinson and Co., London, 1961), while of the wartime books written by a participant, *Spitfire Pilot* by the late David Crook (Faber and Faber, Ltd., London, 1942), is highly commended. Books published in Germany, both during and after the war, are also of varying standards of accuracy and like some of their British counterparts often merely echo previously published accounts.

Publications non-specific to the Battle of Britain but relevant to it and reliable sources of information about the aircraft, squadrons and fighter pilots of the period are *War Planes of The Second World War*, a series by William Green, *Fighter Squadrons of the RAF* by John Rawlings (both published by Macdonald and Co. Ltd., London), and *Aces High* by Christopher Shores and Clive Williams (Neville Spearman Ltd., London, 1966).

Historical and other information about the Bristol Aeroplane Company and Parnall Aircraft, Ltd., together with other background details, were gleaned from inter-war copies of *Flight* magazine (now *Flight International*) and the Bristol *Evening Post*.

KENNETH WAKEFIELD

Glossary of German Terms

The German Air Force – originally the Reichsluftwaffe but better known as the Luftwaffe, its title shortened by popular usage – was based on an organisation and command structure that differed appreciably from that of the Royal Air Force. Thus there are no precise equivalents in the English language to many of the terms used in the Luftwaffe. This is particularly true of ranks and unit designations; a *Staffel*, for example, might be translated as a squadron, but it bears little relationship to an RAF squadron in terms of size or organisation. Accordingly, in the interests of accuracy, German terms are widely used in this book and are listed in the glossary that follows. Luftwaffe ranks, most of which have no direct British translation, are listed separately with their approximate RAF equivalent ranks.

Bf: Bayerische Flugzeugwerke GmbH. Manufacturer of Messerschmitt aircraft (later renamed Messerschmitt A-G).
Beobachter (B): Observer (navigator/bomb-aimer).
Bordfunker (Bf): Wireless Operator/Air Gunner.
Bordmechaniker (Bm): Flight Mechanic/Air Gunner. (Flight Engineer).
Bordschütze (Bs): Air Gunner.
Chef: 'Chief' or officer-in-command.
Do: Dornier-Werke GmbH. Manufacturer of Dornier aircraft.
Eichenlaub: Oak Leaves award (see Ritterkreuz).
Eisernes Kreuz I, II (EK I, II): Iron Cross, First or Second Class.
Ergänzungsstaffel (Erg St): Reserve and Replenishment unit.
Erprobungsgruppe (Erpr Gr): Experimental and Development unit.
Fliegerschule: Flying (pilot) School.
Flugzeugführer (F): Pilot.

Flughafenbetriebskompanie (FBK): Airfield Maintenance and Support Company.

Führungsstab: Operations Staff of the High Command of the Air Force.

Geschwader: Operational unit, approximately equivalent to a Group in the RAF. Normally comprises 3 operational *Gruppen* (which see) and a Staff Flight, with a total establishment of approximately 100 aircraft. Prefixed *Kampf-* (bomber), *Jagd-* (fighter), *Zerstörer-* (long-range fighter), etc., to indicate role.

Geschwaderkommodore (G Kdr): Officer commanding a *Geschwader*.

Geschwaderstab: *Geschwader* Staff HQ.

Gruppe (Gr) : Operational unit, approximately equivalent to a Wing in the RAF. Normally comprises 3 *Staffeln* (which see) and a Staff Flight with a total establishment of approximately 30 aircraft.

Gruppenkommandeur (Gr Kdre): Officer commanding a *Gruppe*.

Gruppenstab: *Gruppe* Staff HQ.

He: Ernst Heinkel Flugzeugwerke. Manufacturer of Heinkel aircraft.

Jagdgeschwader (JG): See *Geschwader*.

Ju: Junkers Flugzeug- und Motorenwerke A-G. Manufacturer of Junkers aircraft.

Kapitän (Kap): See *Staffelkapitän*.

Kampfgeschwader (KG): See *Geschwader*.

Kette: A Section or formation of usually three bomber aircraft.

Kommandant: Commander of a bomber aircraft. Usually the pilot but often the observer.

Kommandeur (Kdre): See *Gruppenkommandeur*.

Kommodore (Kdr): See *Geschwaderkommodore*.

Luftflotte (Lfl): Air Fleet. The largest operational command outside of the German Air Ministry.

Luftkriegsschule: Officer Training School.

Nahkampfführer der Luftwaffe: Air Force Command responsible for close air support of the Army.

Oberkommando der Luftwaffe (OKL): High Command of the Air Force.

Oberkommando der Wehrmacht (OKW): High Command of the Armed Forces.

Reichswehr: German armed forces in the period 1919-1935.

Ritterkreuz (RK): The Knight's Cross of the Iron Cross (in full, *Ritterkreuz des Eisernes Kreuz*). A higher award was the Knight's Cross with Oak Leaves (*Eichenlaub zum Ritterkreuz*).

Seeflieger: Naval airman.

Stab: Staff HQ.

Stabskette: Staff HQ Section of aircraft.

Stabsstaffel (St St): Staff *Staffel* attached to a *Geschwader* HQ.

Staffel (St): Operational unit, approximately equivalent to a Squadron in the RAF. Normally comprised 9 aircraft.

Staffelkapitän (St Kap): Officer commanding a *Staffel*.

Wehrmacht: Armed Forces of the Third Reich (1935-1945), comprising the navy (Kriegsmarine), army (Heer) and air force (Luftwaffe).

Zerstörergeschwader (ZG): See *Geschwader*.

Principal Luftwaffe Ranks with approximate RAF equivalents.

Officers:

Generalfeldmarschall: Marshal of the Royal Air Force

Generaloberst: Air Chief Marshal

General der Flieger: Air Marshal

Generalleutnant: Air Vice Marshal

Generalmajor: Air Commodore

Oberst: Group Captain

Oberstleutnant: Wing Commander

Major: Squadron Leader

Hauptmann: Flight Lieutenant

Oberleutnant: Flying Officer

Leutnant: Pilot Officer

Non-Commissioned Officers (NCOs):

Stabsfeldwebel: Warrant Officer

Oberfeldwebel: Flight Sergeant

Feldwebel: Sergeant

Unteroffizier: Corporal

Other Ranks (ORs):
Obergefreiter: Leading Aircraftman (LAC)
Gefreiter: Aircraftman First Class (AC 1)
Flieger: Aircraftman Second Class (AC 2)

Operational Flying Unit Designations.
Each *Geschwader* was given an identification number (eg, KG 55).
The individual *Staffeln* within the *Geschwader* were numbered 1 to
9 (always using Arabic numbers), with three *Staffeln* in each
Gruppe. Thus, *Staffeln* 1, 2 and 3 formed I Gruppe (the *Gruppen*
always using Roman numerals), with *Staffeln* 4, 5 and 6
comprising II *Gruppe* and *Staffeln* 7, 8 and 9 forming III *Gruppe*. It
follows that 3/KG 55 signifies 3 *Staffel* (within I *Gruppe*) of KG
55, while III/KG55 indicates the third *Gruppe* of the *Geschwader*
(ie, *Staffeln* 7, 8 and 9).

I

Target : Filton

In late September 1940, as the Battle of Britain approached its climax, the German Air Force intensified its attacks against the British aircraft industry. The intention was to prevent Fighter Command making good its losses and in consequence priority for attack went to factories producing fighter aircraft. However, as part of an overall strategy, plants concerned with the manufacture of aero-engines, ancillary equipment and types other than fighters were also included in a list of some thirty major targets to be attacked.

Recent German losses had been of serious proportions and the outcome of the offensive was far from certain. The attempt to eliminate the Royal Air Force, an essential pre-requisite for the proposed invasion of Britain, had developed into a bitter struggle with first one side and then the other appearing to temporarily gain the upper hand. Gradually, however, the scales tipped in favour of the defenders.

The new phase of the Battle brought the Luftwaffe the same mixture of success and failure as before. Some raids on the aircraft factories did little more than add still further to the already heavy losses suffered by the Germans, but on occasion serious damage was inflicted on the British industry. One such occasion occurred on the morning of Wednesday, 25th September, when a large force of escorted bombers attacked the factories of the Bristol Aeroplane Company at Filton, Bristol. It was probably one of the most successful operations of this phase of the Battle of Britain. It was certainly the most daring.

The attack was carefully planned and well executed, but it was also greatly aided by defensive errors of some magnitude. The result was a new and disturbing experience for Bristol, a city that in the early days of the war was considered reasonably safe from bombing attacks. Nevertheless, in view of its importance as a port and as a centre of the aircraft industry, Bristol did not receive evacuees from London and other more probable target cities. Instead it was declared a 'neutral area', which meant it neither received evacuees nor were its own women and children evacuated.

The German attack on Poland opened with heavy attacks by the Luftwaffe against the Polish air force and its aircraft industry, and learning from this the British Air Ministry modified its view of likely targets in Britain. In consequence Bristol was re-assessed as a much more probable target and while there was still no general evacuation, the city's meagre anti-aircraft defences were strengthened. An acute shortage of AA guns prevented much expansion, however, and for some time to come the number available was well below the desired establishment.

Bristol's involvement with the manufacture of aircraft originated in February 1910 when Sir George White, a pioneer of electric tramways and a man of some importance in the commercial life of Bristol, founded the British and Colonial Aeroplane Company, Ltd. At first rented premises were used, but in due course land was acquired at Filton on the northern outskirts of Bristol, and an aerodrome and moderate sized factory were constructed. Within a year extensions to the factory were in hand and some 260 aircraft had been built when the First World War started in 1914. The company's first aircraft, the Box Kite, became well-known but it was a machine built during the war, the F2B Fighter, that established the firm as a leading manufacturer. In 1918 the Filton works produced a record number of 2,000 aircraft, but with the end of hostilities came a drastic cut-back. Nevertheless, in 1919 about 1,000 aircraft emerged from the factory.

On 31st December 1919 the Filton firm changed its trading name to The Bristol Aeroplane Company and shortly afterwards it acquired the ailing Cosmos Engineering Company. Cosmos had been engaged in the development and manufacture of air cooled radial aero-engines and this continued, under the same technical team, when the undertaking was re-located in a large

Filton Aerodrome. A 1931 photograph, with the buildings of the Aero Engine Department in the foreground. Beyond are premises and hangars used by the Bristol Flying School and the Royal Air Force. Expansion of the landing ground to the south and north (left and right in this view) occurred at a later date, and new aero engine buildings were constructed in the foreground. The main aircraft factory is to the left of this photograph, on the south side of the airfield.

building on Filton aerodrome and renamed the Bristol Aero-Engine Department.

The early Twenties were comparatively quiet years, but engine and airframe production and development were at a level that kept the factories busy. The number of employees gradually increased, too, rising from about 700 to nearly 2,500 by 1934. In 1936, with RAF expansion under way, the work force reached 9,000, further soaring to 17,000 by the time of the Munich crisis in 1938. A further substantial increase in 1939 made 'The BAC', as the company was known locally, one of the major employers in the area.

The all-metal Bombay bomber-transport of 1934 and the

Type 134 had paved the way for the Blenheim Mk I, the fastest bomber of its day and one of the first all-metal cantilever monoplanes of stressed skin construction to go into production for the RAF, and this type accounted for most of the company's output in 1938. It was followed in 1939 by the long-nosed Blenheim Mk IV and the Beaufort torpedo-bomber, while work was started on the prototype Beaufighter, a long-range day and, night fighter.

Bristol engine production, too, had increased dramatically, concentrating on both poppet- and sleeve-valved radial engines, and to meet production demands an additional factory, the Rodney Works, was built. The best known Bristol engines included the Mercury, Pegasus and Perseus, and shortly before the outbreak of war these were joined by the Taurus and Hercules. By late 1939 production was centred on the Taurus, Perseus and Hercules, the manufacture of Mercury engines having passed almost entirely to associated Shadow Factories.

Beaufighter production had started by mid-1940 and further expansions of the company were in evidence, developments that did not pass unnoticed by the Luftwaffe's Intelligence Branch, designated 5 Abteilung. When fully expanded company floor space was to cover $2\frac{1}{2}$ million square feet, making it one of the largest aircraft and aero-engine manufacturing plants in the world and one that at its wartime peak employed a work force of 37,000. Directly and indirectly through sub-contracting and Shadow Factories, it produced more than 14,000 military aircraft and 100,000 engines in World War Two.

German knowledge of the Filton complex, nowadays the home of British Aerospace and Rolls-Royce, Limited, was extensive, as revealed in the target briefing documents prepared by 5 Abteilung in 1940. German Air Force Intelligence had divided Filton into three separate but closely associated targets – the aircraft factory, the aero-engine works, and the airfield itself which served both as a factory aerodrome and as an RAF Station.* The German documents were quite detailed and included suitably overprinted maps (based on British Ordnance

---

* The three targets were known respectively to the Luftwaffe as 'GB 74 52 – Werk für Flugzeugzellen Bristol Aero Co. Ltd.', 'GB 73 52 – Motorenfabrik (Schattenwerk) d. The Bristol Aero Co.', and 'GB 10 81 – Fliegerhorst Filton'.

Blenheim Mk IVs in production at Filton.

Blenheim Roll-out. Four Blenheim Mk IVs outside the Flight Sheds at Filton, prior to test flying. The then new aero engine factory at Patchway can be seen in the right background (partially camouflaged) with more Blenheims parked on the airfield awaiting delivery to the RAF. Work is in progress on a tarmac area bounding the taxiway link between the aircraft factory and the airfield (via the railway bridge visible behind the steam-roller). A 1938 photograph.

Patchway. Bristol Perseus engines in production in the 1930s.

Surveys), air photographs, and detailed information sheets. The latter reveal, among other things, a knowledge of the existence of the Beaufighter although at the time it was still on the official Secret List and no details had been released to the public.

One important fact did escape the Germans however – in the autumn of 1940 Filton was also serving as a Fighter Command Sector Station, its Operations Room controlling fighter interceptions over a vital part of the West Country in the recently constituted No 10 Group. No fighters were at that time based on Filton, as had been the case until the spring of that year, but it continued to control the operations of squadrons based at Exeter and Bibury.

Bristol's probable immunity to attack disappeared when the fall of France in June 1940 provided bases from where the German Air Force could strike at almost any target in the British Isles. Almost immediately there began a series of light day and night attacks against the Bristol area where the aircraft factories drew their share of bombs but suffered only minor damage. More serious were the frequent excursions to the air raid shelters and the subsequent loss of production. Between 20th June and 24th September Bristol's sirens sounded 163 air raid Alerts, but

b

Dienstgebrauch

008b/40/016 (Lfl. 3)

vom 27. 9. 40

Filton
Werk für Flugzeugzellen
„The Bristol Aeroplane Co. Ltd."

Länge (westl. Greenw.): 2° 34′ 30″   Breite: 51° 30′ 50″
Mißweisung: — 11° 36′ (Mitte 1940)   Zielhöhe über NN 65 m

Maßstab etwa 1 : 14 600

500   0   500   1000 m

Genst. 5. Abt.   November 1940

Karte 1 : 100 000
GB/E 32

Ⓐ   GB 74 52   Werk für Flugzeugzellen „ The Bristol Aeroplane Co. Ltd. "
Ⓑ   GB 73 52   Flugmotorenfabrik „ The Bristol Aeroplane Co. Ltd. "

GB 74 52. The adjacent housing estates are clearly seen in this photograph of Filton taken in September 1940. Depicting both the aircraft and engine factories, this target photo formed part of the GB 74 52 documentation prepared by the Luftwaffe's 5 Abteilung.

the majority passed without incident; even when bombs did fall the consequences were rarely serious so that in time a potentially dangerous sense of false security was induced. At no time was Bristol attacked by more than a few aircraft and eventually the constantly wailing sirens produced little or no reaction from the public apart from a glance at the sky when AA gunfire was heard. In consequence many factories, including those of the BAC, introduced roof spotters to watch for approaching enemy aircraft and to give a local factory warning when an attack seemed imminent. In this manner normal working was possible through many Alerts with no interference to production.

Such, then, was the general mood of the population and the circumstances governing Alerts when, late in the evening of 24th September, Operations Orders for the following day were drawn up by the GAF's High Command Operations Staff, the Führungsstab of the Oberkommando der Luftwaffe, at its forward headquarters at La Boissière-le-Déluge near Beauvais. Transmitted by teleprinter to the Headquarters of Generalfeldmarschall Hugo Sperrle's Luftflotte 3 at Saint-Cloud near Paris, the Operations Order, which had its origins in the decision taken three weeks earlier to destroy the British aircraft industry, called for a major attack against Target GB 73 52, the aero-engine works of the BAC.

In view of the primary intention to disrupt fighter aircraft production the choice of the BAC engine factory was a strange one, for 5 Abteilung was fully aware that the output of this establishment was mainly concerned with engines for bomber, coastal reconnaissance and trainer aircraft. Yet, unaccountably, at briefing some German airmen participating in the attack were told that the Filton factory was making engines for Spitfires and Hurricanes, despite there being no Intelligence documentation to support this.

The proposed attack was to be carried out by the three operational Gruppen of Kampfgeschwader 55 Greif, the Griffin-Geschwader. Its Heinkel He 111 bombers were to be escorted to and from the target by long-range Messerschmitt Bf 110* two-

---

* The abbreviation 'Me' was widely used by both sides during the war, but throughout this book the official 'Bf' is used in the interests of accuracy.

Filton

Werk für Flugzeugzellen
„The Bristol Aeroplane Co. Ltd."

Geost. 5. Abt. November 1940

Karte 1 : 100 000
GB/E 32

Länge (westl. Greenw.): 2° 34′ 30″   Breite: 51° 30′ 50″
Mißweisung: − 11° 36′ (Mitte 1940)   Zielhöhe über NN 65 m

Maßstab 1:10 560

7452 Werk für Flugzeugzellen „The Bristol Aeroplane Co. Ltd."
1) Fabrikations-u.Montagehallen etwa 30 000 qm
2) Luftschutzunterstände
3) Fabrikationshallen   ˮ   84 000 qm
4) Luftschutzunterstände
5) Neben-u.Lagergebäude etwa   2000 qm
6) Verwaltungsgebäude   ˮ   8000 qm
bebaute Fläche   ˮ   124 000 qm
gesamte Fläche   ˮ   430 000 qm

Target Map. The detailed target map of The Bristol Aeroplane Company's aircraft factory. The Rodney Works are marked "1" and the Patchway engine works are the shaded buildings at top right centre.

seat fighters of Zerstörergeschwader 26, the Horst Wessel Geschwader. Additional protection to just beyond the English coast was to be provided by single-seat Bf 109s with more fighters of this type to meet the bombers and their long-range escort over the coast on their return journey. The Bf 109s, unable to accompany the bombers the whole way because of their limited range, belonged to elements of Jagdgeschwader 2 Richthofen and Jagdgeschwader 53 Pik As, the Ace of Spades Geschwader. Diversionary actions to draw off defending fighters were planned on both flanks of the main assault which was to be preceded by a low level strike against the Portland naval base by Bf 110 fighter-bombers of Erprobungsgruppe 210†, an experimental unit now used in an operational ground attack role.

During the night of 24th/25th September, Bristol experienced another four Alerts. During one of these two He 111s of KG27 bombed what their crews thought was the city, but their bombs fell wide of the target and none landed on Bristol that night. Other aircraft transiting the area reported only mediocre AA gunfire, confirming previous German observations that the city's defences posed no great threat. Perhaps this gave some comfort to the officers planning the mission for the morrow, but the dangers inherent in an inland penetration in daylight were not underestimated and resulted in the carefully conceived plan to outwit the defences.

A reconnaissance flight by a Junkers Ju 88 of 3 (F)/121* on 21st September had revealed that Filton was devoid of fighters and this was confirmed by a second sortie, this time by a Ju 88 of 3 (F)/123, a few days later. Notwithstanding these reports a GAF Intelligence appreciation indicated that up to seventy fighters from other airfields might well be available for the defence of the West Country.

Recent large scale daylight raids over other parts of the country had resulted in heavy losses and in consequence there

---

† A previously published book on the Battle of Britain claims that this unit opened the attack on Filton, acting as 'Pathfinders' for KG55, but this is totally without foundation.

* 3 (F)/121: The 3rd Staffel of Fernaufklärungsgruppe 121, a long-range reconnaissance unit.

Filton

Fliegerhorst Filton

Länge: (westl. Greenw.) 2° 35' Breite: 51° 30'
Mißweisung: –12° (Mitte 1938).

1:63.360 Bl. Nr. 11
1:100.000 Bl. Nr. 32

Stand: Okt. 38

Maßstab 1: 10 560

Filton Airfield. This map formed part of the target documentation for Target No GB 10 81, but also gives details of the aero engine works (Target GB 73 52) and the aircraft factory (GB 74 52). It is based on a British Ordnance Survey map and is dated October 1938.

had been a progressive change to night bombing. It was known, however, that night attacks lacked the precision necessary to destroy a specific objective such as a factory. This was confirmed by the reconnaissance flight of 21st September which revealed just thirteen bomb craters in the vicinity of the Filton works with only slight damage evident in the neighbourhood of the engine test beds. This, from the German viewpoint, was most disappointing in view of the large number of attacks that had been dispatched against the factory during the past three months. The solution, it was hoped, lay in a precision daylight attack by a large force of bombers, their successful penetration of the defences being guaranteed by a substantial fighter escort.

II

For and Against

In the autumn of 1940 the AA defence of the Bristol district rested with the Royal Artillery's 76th Heavy Anti-Aircraft Regiment whose Territorial gunners, with a nucleus of Regular soldiers, manned thirty-two heavy guns equally disposed on eight sites around the city. Their controlling Gun Operations Room at Clifton was connected by telephone to the Filton Sector Operations Room which, in turn, maintained direct communication with No 10 Group Operations Room at Rudloe Manor, Box (near Bath), with No 23 Observer Group Centre in Bristol, and with Fighter Command Headquarters and adjacent Sector Stations. Plots were maintained of all aircraft flying in the area, using information obtained from these centres and other sources within the defence organisation.

The 76th HAA Regiment was formed in 1938 from what was then the 66th (South Midlands) Field Brigade of the Territorial Army and, as Mr S. Phipps, a former member of the regiment, recalls:

> On conversion to AA there was no shortage of volunteers – a common theory in those days was that AA was home defence with not much fear of going overseas. This was true of many units, but was not to be the case with the 76th.*

When embodied on 20th August 1939, the regiment comprised three batteries (236, 237 and 238), but they were ill-equipped. The part-time gunners were initially called-up for a one month training period, but the outbreak of war two weeks later saw

* In October 1942 the 76th HAA Regiment was sent to North Africa and later served in Italy.

their service extended indefinitely. Sid Phipps recalls that he received his telegram ordering him to report to his unit immediately at 7 pm that August evening. He says:

> A hurried search in the coal house for my army gear – and away! Next day we (236 Battery) set up a site at Haberfield, near Pill. We had only two 3-inch guns that were very antiquated, almost museum pieces, and after a few weeks it was decided to see if the guns would fire. As we were only a few hundred yards from Ham Green Hospital we dismantled the sandbag pits and took the guns to the coast at nearby Portishead, fired a few rounds and returned to the site. By Christmas 1939 we were on our concrete pits at Gordano, just a mile or so away. We now had four guns (3·7-inch) per troop (or half-battery), and the peacetime strength was doubled.

The situation had indeed improved by the autumn of 1940 when, in addition to the 76th Regiment's heavy weapons, some 40 mm Bofors guns of 73 Light AA Battery were stationed around Filton. Light AA machine-guns were also installed at certain key points, including some factory rooftops, and on the searchlight sites that ringed the city, but in terms of overall fire power the defences were still woefully weak for a city of Bristol's size and importance.

The control and direction of the defences also left much to be desired, for gun-laying radar was still in its infancy and the great majority of the country's guns were dependent on obsolete sound locators or predictor controlled visual aiming. Early-warning and the tracking of enemy aircraft were also poor by later standards with RDF (Radio Direction Finding), as radar was then known, covering only the sea approaches to the British coasts; over land the tracking of enemy aircraft was a primitive affair that depended almost entirely on the eyes and ears of members of the Observer (later Royal Observer) Corps. Gun-laying (GL) radar equipment was in the offing for Bristol's anti-aircraft guns – indeed Sid Phipps and others were sent on courses of instruction during the first year of the war – but it was not operationally available by September 1940.

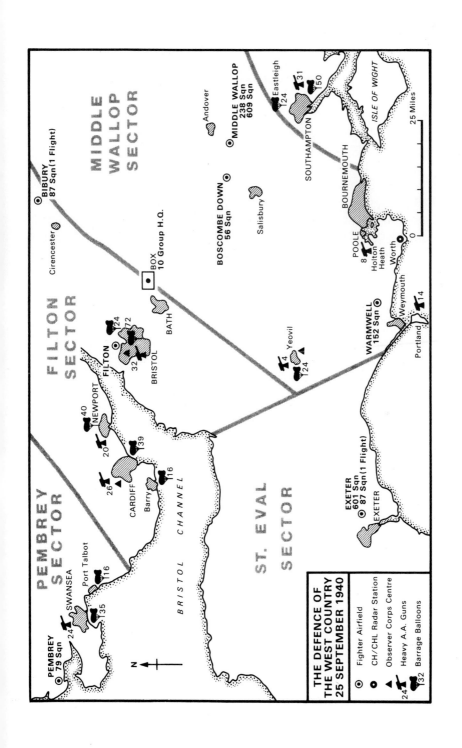

THE DEFENCE OF
THE WEST COUNTRY
25 SEPTEMBER 1940

◉ Fighter Airfield
○ CH/CHL Radar Station
◢ Observer Corps Centre
24⊥ Heavy A.A. Guns
▼32 Barrage Balloons

PEMBREY SECTOR

FILTON SECTOR

MIDDLE WALLOP SECTOR

ST. EVAL SECTOR

PEMBREY
79 Sqn

BIBURY
87 Sqn (1 Flight)

MIDDLE WALLOP
238 Sqn
609 Sqn

BOSCOMBE DOWN
56 Sqn

BOX
10 Group H.Q.

FILTON

BRISTOL

BATH

NEWPORT

CARDIFF

Barry

Port Talbot

SWANSEA

Cirencester

Andover

Salisbury

Yeovil

WARMWELL
152 Sqn

Weymouth

Portland

EXETER
601 Sqn
87 Sqn (1 Flight)

EXETER

Eastleigh

SOUTHAMPTON

BOURNEMOUTH

POOLE

Holton Heath

Worth

ISLE OF WIGHT

BRISTOL CHANNEL

N

0   25 Miles

Barrage balloons were considered an important part of the defence of cities and other vulnerable targets in Britain and to man them special squadrons of the Auxiliary Air Force were formed before the outbreak of war. Intended to prevent accurate low level attacks and dive-bombing, they also forced enemy aircraft to fly at a height at which they could most effectively be engaged by anti-aircraft guns. Unfortunately for the defenders balloons were not available in great numbers – as was the case with AA guns, searchlights and fighter aircraft – but Bristol was provided with what was considered an adequate barrage from the earliest days of the war.

In September 1940 Bristol and its suburbs were protected by ninety-six balloons of the standard LZ type, flown by three squadrons of Balloon Command. These squadrons, former AAF units, were Nos 927 and 951 covering Bristol, and No 935 at Filton; they came under the administrative control of No 11 Balloon Centre at Pucklechurch, near Bristol. With other centres in the south-west, No 11 was part of No 32 (Balloon Barrage) Group, but operational control of all balloon barrages lay with Fighter Command and instructions to raise or lower the barrage normally emanated from the appropriate Sector or Group Operations Rooms.

While the heavy and light anti-aircraft guns, supported by barrage balloons, contributed a great deal to the air defence system of the country, the principal instruments of defence were the fighter aircraft of the Royal Air Force. Under the able command of Air Chief Marshal Sir Hugh Dowding, the RAF's Fighter Command had built up an excellent method of fighter control. Based on then revolutionary techniques involving the use of radar, it was the only system of its type in the world, but shortages of equipment of all types were again in evidence, including a shortage of fighter aircraft.

The day-fighter defence of the West Country in late September consisted of nine squadrons under the control of Air-Vice Marshal Sir Quintin Brand's No 10 Group. Four were equipped with the Hawker Hurricane Mk I, four with the Vickers-Supermarine Spitfire Mk IA, and the other with the obsolete Gloster Gladiator biplane. Although inferior in

Defenders of Bristol. The crew of a 3.7 inch AA gun of 237 Battery, 76th Heavy Anti-Aircraft Regiment, Royal Artillery, on a site at Rockingham Farm, near Avonmouth.

performance to the Bf 109 the Hurricane excelled as a bomber destroyer and was more than a match for the Bf 110. It was thus complementary to the Spitfire which was closely matched to the Bf 109 and superior to anything else the Luftwaffe could put into the air. The Gladiator was another story, but No 247 Squadron which flew this type was then in the St Eval Sector, covering Devon and Cornwall, and together with 234 Squadron, flying Spitfires, was not involved in the attack on Filton.

All of Brand's squadrons had been heavily engaged in the protracted fighting over Britain that summer and some had previously been involved in the Battle for France. Most had

No 10 Group Operations Room The Fighter Command control centre for the West Country at Rudloe Manor, near Box in Wiltshire. It was from here that the overall control of the 10 Group fighters was exercised. The Group Controller from his position in the 'gallery' has an excellent view of the plots of all aircraft flying in his territory. Much of the work in this centre, both plotting and liaison with other centres, was carried out by airwomen of the WAAF.

served in more active sectors before rotation to the West Country and although all were in need of rest, their morale and operational efficiency remained high.

Based in the most active part of 10 Group's territory were the Spitfires of No 152 Squadron, commanded by Squadron Leader Peter K. Devitt and operating from Warmwell in Dorset. Originally formed in the 1914-1918 war, No 152 disbanded in 1919 but reformed again in 1939. In July 1940 it moved south from Acklington, County Durham, and had since been engaged in the struggle for air supremacy over Southern England.

Farther west the former civil airport at Exeter served as a base in the Filton Sector for two Hurricane squadrons, Nos 87 and 601. 87 Squadron maintained one Flight at Bibury Farm airfield, near Cirencester, and as it was mainly engaged on night fighter operations at this time it was not called upon to participate in daylight operations on 25th September. No 601 Squadron, the County of London squadron of the pre-war Auxiliary Air Force, was commanded by Squadron Leader Sir Archibald Hope. Based at Hendon in peacetime, it was sent to France in May 1940 but was withdrawn to England after suffering heavy losses. It became involved in the Battle of Britain from the outset, operating from Tangmere, Debden and Middle Wallop before moving to Exeter, and thus had unrivalled experience of the Luftwaffe.

Another 10 Group Hurricane squadron was No 79, based at Pembrey in South Wales under the command of Squadron Leader J.H. Heyworth. This was another unit with a history dating back to the First World War; disbanded in 1919 it reformed again in 1937 and following the outbreak of war served in France. When the situation there became critical No 79 Squadron was brought back to Britain in preparation for the expected onslaught.

Middle Wallop airfield near Andover was also a Sector Station in 10 Group and housed two day fighter squadrons. One of the resident units was 238 Squadron (Squadron Leader Harold A. Fenton), another First World War squadron that reformed with Hurricanes in 1940 and fought over Southern England and the West Country throughout the Battle of Britain. Middle Wallop's second resident unit was No 609 (West Riding) Squadron (Squadron Leader Horace S. Darley), another former Auxiliary squadron that flew mainly from Northolt and Middle Wallop during that fateful summer. Its Spitfires took a heavy toll of enemy aircraft but the squadron itself suffered severe losses in July. Revenge came, however, on 13th August when, without loss, its pilots claimed thirteen enemy aircraft in one action.

Finally there was No 56 Squadron (Squadron Leader H.M. Pinfold), renowned for its activities in World War One when it numbered among its pilots such famous 'aces' as Ball, McCudden and Rhys-Davids, men who earned the squadron a place of honour in the annals of British military aviation. Between the wars the squadron disbanded and reformed several times, serving in Egypt and Constantinople, but it was in England that it gained further acclaim with its performances at the popular Hendon Air Pageants. In 1938 No 56 Squadron became the third Fighter Command unit to re-equip with Hurricanes and it was with these aircraft that it went to war in France for the second time in twenty-two years. During the summer of 1940 the squadron was busily engaged against the enemy until on 1st September it was declared non-operational and given a few days' rest before resuming operations from Boscombe Down.

Upon these squadrons then, weary but battle proven, rested the fighter defence of Wales and the West Country, a region with many choice targets including ports, industrial centres, aircraft factories and airfields.

In Bristol, as over the entire West Country, Wednesday 25th September dawned fine but slightly hazy, with small amounts of fair-weather cumulus cloud drifting along on a light westerly wind. On such a beautiful morning the war seemed very remote; only the city's barrage balloons nodding gently at their moorings in the parks and other open spaces provided visual evidence that the country was engaged in a bitter struggle for its very existence. Few of the city's early risers, including the many day-shift workers of the Bristol Aeroplane Company, could have imagined that such a day was to bring death and destruction to

A visit by the Commander-in-Chief. Göring in conversation with crews during a visit to KG 55 at Märzdorf/Ohlau airfield, near Breslau, in 1939.

their door-step on a scale not previously experienced in the region, but within a few hours such was to be the case.

Following an early assessment of weather conditions over Great Britain the decision was made to go ahead with the planned attack. A check of aircraft availability revealed that sixty-four He 111s of KG55 and in excess of fifty Bf 110s of ZG26 were serviceable, with a total of fifty-one Bf 109s of I/JG2, II/JG2 and II/JG53. For the low level attack on Portland, the curtain-raiser to the main assault, Erpr Gr 210 could muster eleven Bf 110 fighter-bombers, while the feints on the flanks were to be flown by twenty-three Ju 88s of KG51, detailed to approach Plymouth, with twenty aircraft of the same type belonging to KG54 to make a decoy approach towards Portsmouth. In total, therefore, some 220 aircraft crewed by more than 660 German airmen were involved in the carefully conceived plan.

KG55 came into being in 1937, formed from elements of KG154, KG254 and KG155, and was based at Langendiebach (I

Gruppengefechsstand. The Operations HQ of III Gruppe, KG 55, near Villacoublay.

Gruppe) and Giessen (II Gruppe). In 1939 KG55 was used in the attack on Poland and in December of that year III Gruppe was formed at Neudorf/Oppeln. Subsequently KG55 was deployed against France and with the surrender of that country moved to former Armée de l'Air bases at Chartres, Dreux and Villacoublay. Its pre-war association with Giessen led the *Geschwader* to adopt that town's coat-of-arms as a unit emblem and also resulted in its adoption of the name Griffin Geschwader, the emblem compromising a red and black griffin on a white shield.

The *Geschwaderkommodore*, or overall commander, of KG55 in September 1940 was Oberstleutnant Hans Korte. His *Stabsstaffel* (Staff Flight) aircraft were based at Villacoublay, near Versailles, under the command of Hauptmann Heinz Höfer, and it was near here, at the Château Monteclin, that Korte's *Geschwader* headquarters was located. A key man in this HQ was Major Dr Ernst Kühl, the *Geschwaderstab* Ia (Staff Operations Officer). A most likable man, he was known to his fellow officers as 'Uncle', presumably because he was considerably older than his colleagues. Kühl was largely responsible for the detailed

He 111 P2 of 9/KG 55 based at Villacoublay. This photograph of the G1+LT clearly shows the augmented armament carried by many aircraft of this Geschwader – one additional MG 15 mounted in the roof of the nose section and another, mounted to fire forward, in the Bola below the fuselage. The observer can be seen in the prone position manning the nose (A-Stand) armament. The undersurfaces of the wings and fuselage retain large areas of the black distemper applied for night operations and not always removed for daylight attacks.

planning of KG55's operations and participated in many of them, as he did in the attack on Filton.

It was usual practice in the Luftwaffe at this time for the *Geschwaderkommodore*, a senior officer commanding the equivalent of an RAF Bomber Group, to take part in operational missions and already KG55 had lost one *Kommodore*, Oberst Alois Stöckl, over England. For the attack on Filton Oberstleutnant Korte, Stöckl's successor, was to follow this custom, flying with his *Stabskette*, a section of aircraft belonging to the *Geschwader* Staff Flight. Another machine of the *Stabskette* was to be flown by Oberleutnant Wilhelm Antrup, the *Geschwaderstab* Technical Officer, then thirty years old and destined to become one of the outstanding bomber pilots of World War Two.

Sharing Villacoublay airfield with Korte's *Stabsstaffel* was III Gruppe under the command of Major Hans Schemmell and it was with this *Gruppe* that the Staff Flight aircraft usually flew on operations. I Gruppe, commanded by Hauptmann Joachim

Roeber, was based at Dreux with II Gruppe, led by Major Friedrich Kless, at Chartres. A breakdown of the organisation of the *Geschwader* and a listing of its senior officers is to be found in Appendix I.

At the beginning of the campaign in the West KG55 possessed 108 He 111s, but by 7th September, despite a flow of replacement aircraft, its strength had diminished to sixty-eight. Its level of operations imposed a great deal of work on the *Flughafenbetriebskompanien* (FBK), the aircraft maintenance companies attached to KG55, who were hard pressed to keep the bombers under their care fully serviceable. The intensity of operations had also affected the appearance of the *Geschwader*'s aircraft, for during the summer of 1940 there had been little opportunity to keep the finish of the machines immaculate, as had been the case formerly. In addition, night operations had seen the application of a black distemper over the Heinkels' pale blue undersurfaces and, in some cases, in irregular patches over much of their two-tone dark green upper surfaces. Nationality, unit and individual aircraft lettering were also often blacked out in an attempt to give protection from the prying beams of searchlights. This temporary night flying finish resembled lampblack and was intended to be washed off for daylight operations, but due to pressure of work on the FBK personnel this was seldom done and many machines taking part in the attack on Filton continued to wear their sombre night finish, in total or in part. The result was a somewhat motley collection of aircraft, with only the Griffin insignia to identify some machines with their parent *Geschwader*.

In contrast the Bf 110s of ZG26 were colourful in the established tradition of German fighter aircraft. Named after Horst Wessel, the young Nazi martyr, ZG26 was one of the élite 'Destroyer' units charged by Göring with wresting air superiority from the RAF over its own territory. The *Zerstörer* units, all equipped with Bf 110s by the autumn of 1940, had gained an enhanced reputation over Poland, Norway, France and the Low Countries, but the heavy twin-engined fighters were outclassed by the Spitfire and although faster than the Hurricane lacked the latter's superb manoeuvrability. They did,

(Left) Oberstleutnant Joachim-Friedrich Huth, Geschwaderkommodore of ZG 26. (Right) Hauptmann Wilhelm Makrocki, Kommandeur of I/ZG 26.

(Left) Hauptmann Hans Schalk, Kommandeur of III/ZG 26. (Right) Hauptmann Ralph von Rettburg, Kommandeur of II/ZG 26.

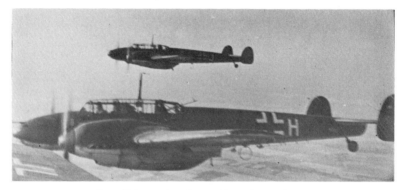

Escort Fighters – Long Range. Bf 110 C4s of 3/ZG 26.

however, possess a lethal forward firing armament comprising two 20 mm MG FF cannon and four 7·9 mm MG 17 machine-guns, with a single MG 15 manned by the wireless operator in the rear cockpit.

ZG 26 had fought most of the Battle of Britain under the direction of Jafu 2, operating over south-east England, but in September the *Geschwader* was placed under the control of Jafu 3 for operations with V Fliegerkorps over the south of England including the Western Counties. Its *Geschwaderkommodore* was Oberstleutnant Joachim Huth, a highly respected and popular airman who had lost a leg in World War One and who was a holder of the *Ritterkreuz*, the Knight's Cross of the Iron Cross. His *Gruppe* commanders were Hauptmann Wilhelm Macroki, Hauptmann Ralph von Rettburg and Hauptmann Hans Schalk, commanding I, II and III Gruppen respectively. Their new theatre of operations demanded base changes and in September the three *Gruppen* moved into airfields at Cherbourg, Le Havre and Thiberville.

There was a lack of standardisation in the unit code markings carried by the Bf 110s of Zerstörergeschwader 26. Originally allocated the code 'U8', which was painted in black to the left of the black cross on the side of their aircraft, ZG 26 was later given the code '3U'. The change was not immediately implemented in the field, however, and for a long time – certainly until well after the Battle of Britain period – aircraft belonging to the *Geschwader*

Escort Fighter – Short Range. A Bf 109 E of the Guernsey-based 4/JG 53. Aircraft of this unit provided cover to the English coast for the He 111s of KG 55 on 25th September 1940. A rare photograph of a German fighter in the German occupied Channel Islands.

bore either code. In the main, at least in September 1940, the aircraft of I Gruppe carried the markings U8 while those of II and III Gruppen predominantly wore 3U. The camouflage finish of the aircraft varied, too, the earlier variants of the Bf 110 Cs carrying a two-tone dark green upper surface finish while later C-variants had mottled fuselage sides. Various tactical finishes were also employed, a removeable white distemper being used, for example, on the nose section of aircraft belonging to III Gruppe. In all cases the undersurfaces of the fuselage, wings and tailplane were finished in the standard *Hellblau*, a light blue colour adopted by the Luftwaffe for nearly all its operational aircraft.

The single-seat, highly efficient but short range Bf 109 Es were destined to play only a minor role in the operation under review and because of this it is not intended to examine these single-engined fighter units in detail. It is of interest to note, however, that among the pilots flying with JG2 on this occasion were Major Helmut Wick and Oberfeldwebel Werner Machold, two of the Luftwaffe's then top scoring 'aces', credited with thirty and twenty-one 'kills' respectively. Beyond this it will suffice to record that the participating Bf 109 Es were based at Beaumont-le-Roger (I and II/JG2), and on landing grounds in Brittany and on the island of Guernsey (II/JG53), and that all three *Gruppen* possessed a wealth of combat experience.

III

To the Normandy Coast

The Operations Order for the attack on Filton, transmitted by teleprinter from the *Geschwaderstab* HQ, only reached the three *Gruppe* commanders on the morning of the 25th although Friedrich Kless, casting his mind back, thinks it possible that he received a provisional warning at his II Gruppe headquarters late the previous evening. Certainly, however, no actual order detailing the operation was received until early on the day of the attack when confirmation had been obtained of favourable weather in the Bristol area. Thus, only as the city of Bristol came to life that September morning did preparations get under way on the airfields at Chartres, Dreux and Villacoublay.

At Chartres/Oiseme – and events here were typical of those at the other two airfields – the officers commanding the three *Staffeln* comprising II Gruppe were summoned to their *Gruppenkommandeur* at 07.00 hours German Time (06.00 in Britain, then keeping British Summer Time*). At the same time an initial warning of the impending operation was given to aircrew personnel billeted in the village of Oiseme.

Karl Gerdsmeir, then a flight mechanic/gunner with 5 Staffel, recalls that shortly after this warning he and his colleagues were taken to the airfield in trucks. By the time they arrived the ground crews were already preparing the aircraft and to pass the time the flying crews assisted them, checking over the guns and ammunition and generally making themselves useful. After a while they were called for a briefing by their *Staffelkapitän*,

---

* From here on all times are given in British Summer Time (BST) unless otherwise stated.

Hauptmann Gabriel, now back from his meeting with the *Gruppe* commander at the *Gefechtsstand*, the *Gruppe* Operations HQ. In the meantime fuel requirements and details of the bomb loads had been passed to the mechanics and armourers; other ground crew members were busy with final checks of the aircraft and their equipment while others were given the job of removing the black distemper temporary night flying finish from the undersurfaces of the bombers, a dirty and unpopular task.

Unteroffizier Gerdsmeier's *Staffelkapitän* opened the briefing by stating that the attack was part of a new phase in the air war. Its aim, he said, was the destruction of the British aircraft industry and in particular that part of it concerned with fighter production. This made good sense to Karl Gerdsmeier and his fellow crew members; indeed, they were of the opinion that such a step was long overdue. Filton, they were told, albeit erroneously, was producing Rolls-Royce engines for Spitfires and Hurricanes and the destruction of this plant would be a major blow to the RAF.

To aid target-finding Kampfgeschwader 55 was to follow the common German practice of first proceeding to an easily recognisable landmark close to the intended objective. This provided a reference point from where to start the bombing run and for this attack Weston-super-Mare, unmistakable on the Somerset* coast of the Bristol Channel, was chosen. The route from the bomber assembly point over Normandy was to Cherbourg, for the rendezvous with the fighter escort, and thence direct to Weston-super-Mare with Portland Bill a prominent en route check point. In attacks of this type the ground features between the target and the nearby well-defined landmark were carefully studied by the attack leader and his deputies, but in this instance the approach was made simple by the close proximity of the Bristol Channel coastline that paralleled the track to the target. Any attempt to bring a large, unwieldy formation around for a second run-in would have been

---

* Place names and county boundaries are given here as they existed in 1940 and no account has been taken of recent revisions.

Karl Gerdsmeier and (right) Gerdsmeier in the cockpit of his He 111.

both difficult and dangerous, but the usual method of approach had worked well in the past and, besides aiding the bombing run, helped to disguise the intended target until almost the last moment. An essential requirement though was good visibility with little or no cloud, for an inability to see the target throughout the bombing run would almost certainly jeopardise the entire operation.

At briefing crews were shown a recent air photograph of the Filton complex and it was pointed out that while the buildings were heavily camouflaged, their location was aided by the pattern of adjacent railway lines. The briefing went on to cover the known positions of flak batteries, balloon sites and fighter airfields. The route to and from the target and communications procedures were discussed and crews were given details of the fighter escort and the proposed diversionary actions. Pilots were additionally given a detailed description of the formation to be flown with their precise position in that formation, to facilitate the link-up with the other two *Gruppen* near Evreux while en route to Cherbourg. The weather was forecast to be good over the entire route with a maximum of 7/10ths cloud over France decreasing to little or none at all over the English Channel and only small amounts of cumulus over England. At this many present felt some misgivings – good weather, they knew, was essential for such an attack, but it promised an uncomfortable reception by the 'Tommies'. There was, however, some optimism because of the decoy actions planned on the flanks, and the fighter escort to be provided sounded encouraging. Nevertheless, no attempt was made to make light of the task ahead and to cover all eventualities crews were given several alternative targets, the first being the Portland naval base.

Gerdsmeier fully appreciated the potential hazards facing them for on 16th August during a similar *Geschwader* attack on the Fairey Aviation Works at Feltham and nearby Heathrow airfield, he had lost several close friends. On that occasion, while Spitfires engaged escorting Bf 109s, more British fighters came sweeping in to attack the bombers. In close proximity to Gerdsmeier's aircraft was the G1+LM*, a He 111 of 4 Staffel that numbered among its crew four of his friends, men with whom he had regularly flown in the past and with whom even now he spent much of his spare time.

One of them, Bordmechaniker Erich Schmidtke, had told Karl Gerdsmeier before take-off that he was not happy with the position they had been allocated in the formation. They were to occupy the unpopular '*Katschmarek*' position in the rearmost outer formation so often singled out for attention by British fighters. Schmidtke had remarked to Gerdsmeier that, in his view, it would be a miracle if they ever met again and his prophecy was to come true. Approaching Aldershot, with its bombs still on board, the G1+LM was hit and blew up. There was an enormous flash and only a smudge of dirty black smoke remained to mark the end of five men and their aircraft.

---

* The *Geschwader* code G1 was carried on all aircraft of KG55; the first letter to the right of the black cross (*Balkenkreuz*) indicated the individual aircraft and the last letter its *Staffel*.

Gerdsmeier was never to forget that sight and then, as now, the skies over Britain were practically clear. Two more Heinkels failed to return from that attack, the first flown over England by KG55 at full *Geschwader* strength, and many were damaged.

Within the hierarchy of KG55 there was probably an even greater appreciation of the dangers to be faced.

> It was clear to us that it was a risky attack, for by this time we knew that the English fighter defence was based on a radar system that functioned well. Our hopes lay with the expectation that the focal point of the fighter defence would be centred on the Greater London area.

Thus the former *Gruppenkommandeur* of II/KG55 to the author. Friedrich Kless continued:

> From the English coast to Bristol we had only the *Zerstörer* Messerschmitt 110 escort and in total we viewed our fighter protection as feeble in the extreme.

As a *Gruppe* commander Kless was burdened with administrative and other ground duties, but he nevertheless flew on all the operational missions undertaken by his *Gruppe* and was in an unequalled position to assess the difficulties and the possible outcome of the proposed attack. As will be seen, he was to play a vital role in the Filton operation and accordingly some details of his background and military service are of some relevance.

Born in 1906 in Bayreuth, Bavaria, Friedrich Kless entered the Reichswehr at the age of eighteen and during his career was appointed Inspecting Officer at the Kriegsschule Dresden, attended the Kriegsakademie, and transferred to the Luftwaffe in 1938. He trained as a pilot/observer and in 1939 was appointed to 5 Fliegerdivision as Ia (Staff Operations Officer) to Generalmajor Ritter von Greim. With the German offensive in the West, Kless became the Ia of the Nahkampfführer der Luftwaffe, involved with the close air support of Guderian's Panzerkorps during its phenomenal break-through to the

Channel Coast. At the end of May 1940 he became *Kommandeur* of II/KG55 and flew in the latter part of the French campaign and then in day and night operations over Britain.

From the recent triumphs at Sedan and Calais the war of Friedrich Kless suddenly took a very different turn. His brother had also followed an air force career and as a *Major* commanded III/KG77 in the Battle of Britain, but on 18th September Max Kless was killed when his Ju 88 was shot down during a daylight attack on the London docks. Now, only a week later and with the death of his only brother still much in his thoughts, Friedrich Kless was to lead not only his *Gruppe* but the entire *Geschwader* on a similar mass daylight raid.

Kless's II Gruppe was regarded as the most experienced and most proficient of KG55's three *Gruppen* and accordingly it was selected to occupy the leading centre position of the *Geschwader* formation, flanked by the other two *Gruppen*. Kless, trained as both a pilot and observer, was to fly on this occasion in the latter capacity, assuming responsibility for the navigation and bomb aiming of the lead aircraft and thus the entire *Geschwader*. With Kless in operational command of the attack, Hans Korte, Kless's commanding officer, was to fly on this occasion on the right flank, his *Stabskette* attaching itself to III Gruppe in a subordinate position.

Like many other former KG55 crew members Karl Gerdsmeier well remembers the halcyon days of mid-summer 1940, a time of unparalleled German military success culminating with the signing of the Armistice with France. On that day the entire *Geschwader* participated in a show of might, flying low over the railway coach in the Forest of Compiègne where the French delegation was summoned for the meeting with Hitler and his entourage. Gerdsmeier recalls:

> During our low fly-past we could clearly see the German troops, lined up as a guard of honour, and the famous railway coach, brought to Compiègne from Paris for the occasion. After the flight we landed at either Bourges or Rouen – I

forget which – and remained there for the night, sleeping in tents. The next day we flew on to Villacoublay but again only remained there for one day before the three *Staffeln* of II Gruppe were moved to Chartres.

When we arrived the town was deserted. The civil population had, for the most part, flown. After a few days our vehicles arrived, packed with bedding and other items. The officers were quartered in a nearby château and the NCOs and ORs, aircrew and ground personnel, were accommodated in the village of Oiseme, close to the airfield. Three crews, my own included, were billeted in a small house in which we found all the cupboards boarded-up. The occupier, a Frenchman who spoke good German, visited us often and progressively removed his belongings from the sealed cupboards.

Other crews lived in a school and in other houses and only the sentries on guard duty remained on the airfield. When an operation was to take place a messenger was sent to us, his usual cry being '*Fertigmachen zum Einsatz!*' – 'Get ready for an operation!'

By the day of the Filton attack we knew that other accommodation had been arranged for us; in the town there was a large building, formerly a school of domestic science, and this was requisitioned for us. The advantages were twofold – it was fitted with central heating and possessed large kitchens. Until now our meals had been prepared in a field kitchen on Chartres airfield and were brought to us in the village or alternatively we were required to attend the airfield at mealtimes.

Thus, despite Gerdsmeier's misgivings about the day ahead, the future in general looked somewhat brighter with the promise of better things to come in terms of creature comfort. He was even more gladdened, however, by the knowledge that the very next day he was due to go on leave and, in anticipation, his kit was already packed for the long awaited return to his home in Germany.

By the time crew briefing was over the ground crews had finished refuelling and bombing-up. For the most part the bombs were high explosive SC 50s, SC 250s and delayed action SC 250 LZZs, all thin-cased weapons with a high charge/weight ratio for maximum blast effect. As their designation implies, they fell into two weight categories, 50 kg (110 pounds) and 250 kg (550 pounds), light by later standards but effective weapons nevertheless. In addition some aircraft were loaded with Flam C 250 oil-filled incendiary bombs, similar in size and appearance to the SC 250 but lighter in weight. Although generally effective these so-called oil bombs had a tendency to break-up on impact and were not the most reliable weapons in the German armoury. On the whole, however, German weapons and equipment, including their aircraft, were most reliable although British propaganda had been remarkably successful in convincing the public to the contrary. German aircraft and crews, it was confidently believed, were in every way inferior to those of the Royal Air Force. There were constant references in newspaper reports to German aircraft lacking even basic flight instruments and being manned by 'seventeen year old Nazis', but in truth most German aircraft and crews were on a par with their opposite numbers in the RAF. Perhaps the weakest aspect of the German bombers in use in 1940 was their defensive armament, but this was offset to some extent by modifications introduced in the field and subsequently incorporated on production lines.

Morale in the Luftwaffe was good, as was to be expected in an air force that until now had known only the sweet taste of success. Its standards of training and initial selection produced capable crews and, contrary to propaganda-orientated British reports, their aircraft used little *ersatz* material, were soundly designed, and were extremely well built. In general there was little to choose between the two air forces; perhaps the numerical superiority of the German Air Force should have given it the advantage but, in the end, it was the British early-warning radar, tied to an efficient fighter control system, that tipped the scales in favour of the RAF. From time to time, however, the balance wavered to the tip in favour of the Luftwaffe, and such an event occurred on the morning of 25th September.

Karl Gerdsmeier's He 111.

At about 09.00 hours BST Gerdsmeier and his fellow crew
members climbed aboard the G1+DN through the hinged hatch
in the lower gun position. Known as the Bola (from *Bodenlafette*,
the lower gun-mounting) this ventral gun position was officially
termed the C-Stand and in flight was normally manned by the
Bordmechaniker or flight mechanic. In addition to Gerdsmeier, a
26-year-old NCO who had been in the Luftwaffe since 1935, the
crew comprised a pilot, observer, wireless operator and gunner.
Gerdsmeier, the *Bordmechaniker*, had been with the Boelcke
Geschwader before joining KG55 and had been with his present
crew since March 1940. In his view every man in the crew was a
'master of his job'. His pilot, and also the aircraft *Kommandant*,
was Oberleutnant Gottfried Weigel, assessed by Gerdsmeier
who had flown with many pilots as 'a good airman who
subscribed to a policy of Safety First'. An experienced pilot and
officer, Weigel also served as deputy to his *Staffelkapitän*,
Hauptmann Hans-Joachim Gabriel.

Gerdsmeier's aircraft, the 'Dora Nordpol' in the Luftwaffe's
phonetic alphabet, included in its crew two senior NCOs,

Behind German Lines. Oberleutnant Weigel's He 111 is inspected by German soldiers and airmen after crash landing behind the advancing German army in Belgium, 13th May 1940. Oberleutnant Weigel can be seen on the port wing (in peaked cap with hand raised).

Oberfeldwebel Alfred Narres, observer (navigator/bomb aimer), and Feldwebel Georg Engel, wireless operator/gunner. The latter had also been in the air force since 1935 and like the rest of the crew had participated in the French campaign. In the course of this, on their third flight of the day on 13th May, they were shot down by French Morane Saulnier MS 406 fighters, but Weigel managed to make a forced landing at Attern in Belgium, behind the German lines, and the crew thus evaded capture.

The fifth member of Gerdsmeier's crew was gunner Karl Geib, holding only the rank of *Gefreiter* - equivalent to an AC1 in the RAF – but already a veteran with twenty-three operational flights over France and, to date, eighteen over Britain. Aged twenty-one, Geib was the youngest member of the crew while Narres, who was nearly thirty, was the oldest. In terms of age and experience this crew was typical of those operating over Britain at that time, but there were exceptions, one such being the crew of Oberleutnant Speck von Sternberg.

Speck von Sternberg's crew was unusual in that his observer, Oberfeldwebel Martin Reiser, was forty-two years old. Born in

Veteran observer. Feldwebel Martin Reiser in the A-Stand position of a He 111 of 9/KG 55. Reiser flew against Britain in both World Wars and took part in the attack on Filton on 25th September 1940.

Brandstätt in 1898, Reiser was not only the oldest aircrew member of his *Gruppe* but was unique in that he had flown operationally against Britain in both world wars. After service as a young sailor in a sail training ship he joined the Kaiserliche Marine in 1917 and after initial training and training with I Seeflieger-Abteilung Kiel/Holtenau flew as an observer in the Ago floatplanes of Kampfstaffel Höpken, based at Ostend under Seeflieger-Flandern and carrying out patrols off the south-east coast of England. By the end of the war Reiser held the rank of *Maat* and had completed a dozen or so operational flights, for which he was awarded the Iron Cross 2nd Class. He returned to civilian life, but in 1937, as an *Unteroffizier der Reserve*, he was called to attend a refresher course as an *FT/Beobachter* (wireless operator/observer) at the Seefliegerschule (See) Parow, the Reichsluftwaffe now expanding rapidly under the Hitler régime. He went back to his restaurant business after three months, but in 1939 was again called to serve the Fatherland, leaving behind a wife and newly born daughter. After training at Illesheim and

Leutnant Tüffers.

Krakau with 1/Erg KG 3 he attended the Luftkriegsschule Klotzsche and was posted to 9/KG 55 at Villacoublay in July 1940. In 1918 he had been the youngest airman in his unit; now, twenty-two years later, he discovered he was the oldest.

Martin Reiser's pilot, Oberleutnant Johannes Speck von Sternberg, was also the *Staffelkapitän* of 9/KG 55, and in this crew Reiser found himself among experienced but much younger men. The *Staffelkapitän* was twenty-seven years old and the second oldest member of the crew while wireless operator Gefreiter Rudolf Budde, who was twenty-two years Reiser's junior, was the youngest. Johannes Speck was much respected by Reiser and it appears that the feeling was mutual. The older man had a meticulous approach to his work; he had lost the recklessness of youth and with his wide experience of life and two world wars, no doubt brought a degree of maturity to the crew. He was a staunch patriot, determined to give of his best for his country, and realised that only the defeat of Britain would enable him to return to his family and his restaurant.

Preparing for Take Off. He 111s of III/KG 55 taxi out for take off from Villacoublay. In the foreground the G1+CT of 9 Staffel.

Crew boarding an He 111 at Villacoublay.

Accordingly he was determined to do his utmost to help bring this about, and with all possible speed.

The attack on Filton was to be Martin Reiser's fourteenth operational flight of World War Two and his second *Geschwader*-strength attack, the first having been against Heathrow/Feltham on 16th August. On that occasion he had been flying in the G1+HT commanded by Leutnant Tüffers. They were badly shot up by fighters and with the flight mechanic wounded in the chest and leg, and flying on one engine, they limped back to France, escorted by two Bf 110 fighters. After landing safely they counted thirty-five bullet holes in the airframe of the He 111, with more in the propellers and tyres. For the attack now in the offing Reiser, a keen photographer, decided to take his camera to record for posterity a *Geschwader* attack on England. He sensed it would be a day to remember.

Exactly on time Oberleutnant Weigel started the motors of his Heinkel and started to taxi to the downwind boundary of Chartres airfield preparatory to a formation take off. From 09.24 onwards, with the French countryside reverberating to the roar of Daimler Benz engines developing full power, the heavily laden bombers of II Gruppe took off. Climbing slowly they swept around in a wide turn, the three aircraft of each *Kette* easing into *Staffel* and then *Gruppe* formation as, led by the *Gruppen-kommandeur* in the G1+AC, course was set for Evreux and the rendezvous with the other two *Gruppen*.

With a slightly greater distance to cover from Villacoublay to the rendezvous area the three *Staffeln* of III Gruppe were airborne a little earlier, the log book of Oberleutnant Werner Oberländer, the pilot of the G1+HR of 7 Staffel, revealing his take off time as 09.16. Provided that all went according to plan, Oberländer expected to be back at Villacoublay after a flight of some four hours, but while optimistic of the outcome, he, too, was under no illusions about the dangers that lay ahead. He had little time to dwell upon such things however, for all his attention was centred on formating on his *Staffelkapitän*, Oberleutnant Hans Bröcker, flying the G1+LR.

Oberländer, making his 38th operational flight, had carried

Werner Oberländer. The pilot of a He 111 in the attack on Filton, Oberländer was awarded the Ritterkreuz in 1943. He was seriously wounded in Russia while participating in his 263rd operational flight.

out attacks on the Bristol area several times in recent weeks, both by day and night. Another experienced pilot he had started his flying career in 1932 at the age of nineteen and before joining III/KG 55 had served as an instructor at the Luftkriegsschule, Dresden. Like so many of his colleagues, his optimism with regard to this operation was based on a confidence inspired by sound training, long experience, and a high degree of faith in his colleagues and air force commanders.

However, few if any of the German airmen heading towards Bristol that morning had other than the highest respect for the British fighter pilots who, they suspected, would be waiting for them, determined to defend their island homeland with their usual courage and skill.

Already, though, the strength of the German bomber force was reduced by one aircraft. A technical problem on take-off forced Hans Korte's Heinkel to abort, bringing to an abrupt end the *Kommodore*'s intended participation in the attack.

He 111Ps of 9/KG 55, Villacoublay. It is believed that this well known photograph was taken on the day of the major attack on Filton.

The assembly of a large number of heavily laden bombers was not an easy task, but the tactical formations adopted by the Luftwaffe were designed to eliminate some of the problems while providing a grouping that afforded both good cross-fire protection against enemy fighters and a compact 'bomb fall' pattern.

The basic German bomber formation was the section or *Kette* of three aircraft in the familar 'V'-shape, and various combinations of the basic formation were available to suit operations at *Staffel*, *Gruppe* or *Geschwader* strength. Take-off for daylight formation raids were normally made in *Kette* or *Staffel* strength, depending on the size of the airfield in use; take-offs in larger groups, although simplifying subsequent assembly, were often impractical and potentially too dangerous.

Despite all the problems of assembling a large number of aircraft from three bases, the sequence went exactly as planned and the three *Gruppen* met up over Evreux and continued on course for Cherbourg, slowly climbing to 5,000 metres (16,400 feet).

The formation assembly and the flight to Cherbourg took about 1¾ hours and as the Heinkels came up overhead the Peninsula at 11.00 hours their crews could see the Bf 110 escort fighters climbing to join them. Contrary to the expected partly cloudy conditions in this area the sky was clear with excellent visibility.

The Bf 110s took up a position above and to the rear of the bombers, climbing to 19,000 feet and weaving gently to maintain station with their slower charges which were stepped up from 15,000 to 16,000 feet in *Ketten* of three aircraft. The three *Staffeln* of each *Gruppe* themselves formed a large 'V' and the entire force took up what was known as a *Geschwaderkeil*, three huge arrow heads with I Gruppe on the left flank, II Gruppe leading in the centre, and III Gruppe to the right. The Bf 109s ranged far ahead, out of sight of the main formation, with the intention of sweeping the skies clear of British fighters over the coast. As usual they were in sections of two or, more usually, four machines, the well known 'finger four' later adopted by most of the world's air forces. The Bf 110s, flying to the rear of the bombers in sections of four or five aircraft in loose line astern, provided top and rear close cover.

This then, was the composition of the German force when RDF contact was first made by the British. The time was 11.04.

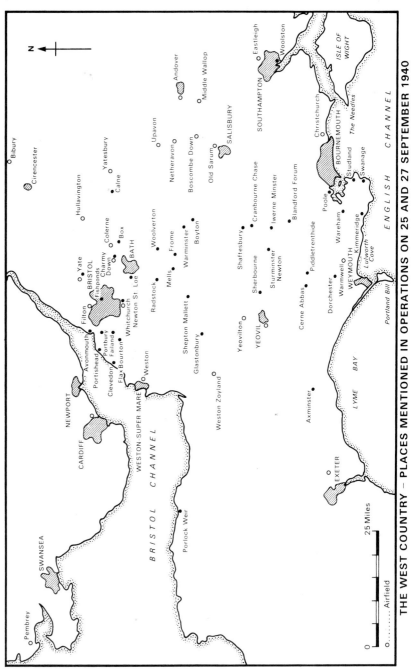

THE WEST COUNTRY – PLACES MENTIONED IN OPERATIONS ON 25 AND 27 SEPTEMBER 1940

IV

Confusion in Defence

The tranquillity of the quiet, gently rolling countryside was shattered as two Spitfires of 152 Squadron sped across the undulating grass surface of Warmwell, an airfield nestling in the Dorset countryside a few miles inland from Weymouth. When safely airborne the two Spitfires executed a climbing turn eastwards and set off to patrol the Isle of Wight at 20,000 feet. The remainder of the squadron's pilots were termed 'Available', a state of preparedness for action that required them to be able to take off, or 'scramble' in Fighter Command parlance, at fifteen minutes' notice. Most of the other squadrons in No 10 Group were similarly Available and only one unit in the entire Group, No 609 at Middle Wallop, was at Readiness and prepared to take off at a moment's notice.

The first RDF plots of the approaching 'Bandits' appeared on the plotting tables in the Command, Group and Sector Operations Rooms following reports from the coastal Chain Home Stations. Designated 'Raid 22', a force of ten aircraft, the plotting room symbols showed the raid off Cherbourg, heading towards Portland.

The reported strength of Raid 22, based on the size of the radar response or echo and not a precise estimate at long range, caused no undue concern at Group Headquarters as no scramble was ordered, but at 11.07 hours the status of 152 Squadron was changed from Available to Readiness, as a precaution. While this was happening the size of Raid 22 was amended to Ten Plus and two minutes later No 609 Squadron at Middle Wallop was ordered to scramble with instructions to patrol Swanage at 20,000 feet.

At 11.11 hours all available fighters at Exeter were also prudently brought to Readiness and 152 Squadron was ordered to take off and climb to 20,000 feet over Portland. This followed improved radar returns which resulted in re-assessments of Raid 22's strength; from here onwards the estimated strength increased progressively until, approaching the English coast, the enemy force was plotted as Sixty Plus, a far cry from the original estimate of ten aircraft.

By now there must have been some concern at Group Headquarters with, at 11.15, the raiders only 18 miles south-south-east of Portland and still no 10 Group squadrons airborne; only the two Spitfires of 152 Squadron were in the air and they, at this moment, were over the Isle of Wight at 20,000 feet. Eventually at 11.18 and with the enemy only 5 miles east of Portland Bill, No 609 squadron became airborne from Middle Wallop, nine minutes after Group had issued the order to take-off. This was an exceptionally long time to get airborne, the average scramble time in Fighter Command being about four minutes. Heading for Swanage as instructed the squadron was subsequently re-vectored towards Portland, but by now the German aircraft were about to cross the Dorset coast.

At about this time the decoy Ju 88s of KG 54 entered the picture, as did those of KG 51 off Plymouth, while the eleven Bf 110s of Erpr Gr 210 came sweeping in at low level. Each fighter-bomber was carrying two SC 500 bombs and coming in at high speed they delivered their attack at 11.20, opposed only by innaccurate light AA fire. Turning onto a southerly heading they sped back out to sea to return to their base at Cherbourg without loss. Their crews subsequently reported hitting their target, the Portland naval base, but they were unable to assess the results of the bombing. They had, in fact, damaged a few oil tanks, brought down some telephone wires, blocked the main road to Portland and destroyed fifteen houses, but fortunately there were no casualties.*

While this attack was in progress the now almost certainly somewhat harassed 10 Group Controller ordered 601 Squadron's Hurricanes at Exeter to take off and proceed to

---

* A previously published account of the Battle of Britain states that the attack on Portland was made by Ju 88s of LG 1, but a detailed account of the operation exists in German records and contradicts this suggestion.

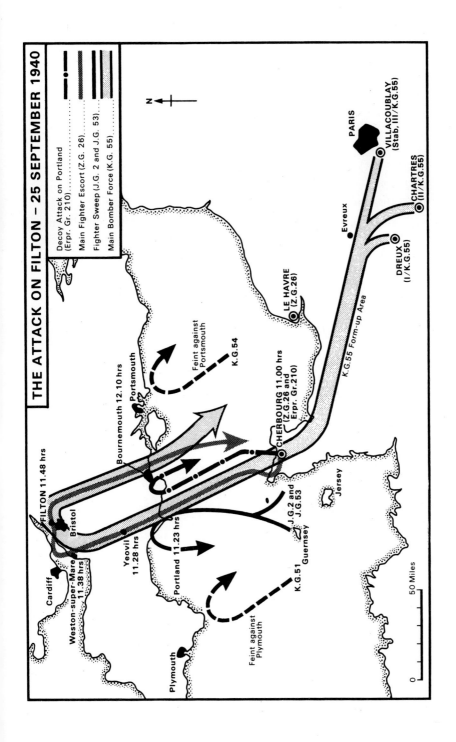

THE ATTACK ON FILTON – 25 SEPTEMBER 1940

Decoy Attack on Portland (Erpr. Gr. 210)......
Main Fighter Escort (Z.G. 26)......
Fighter Sweep (J.G. 2 and J.G. 53)......
Main Bomber Force (K.G. 55)......

N

Cardiff

Weston-super-Mare 11.38 hrs

FILTON 11.48 hrs
Bristol

Bournemouth 12.10 hrs

Yeovil 11.28 hrs

Portland 11.23 hrs

Plymouth

Feint against Plymouth

K.G.51

Guernsey
Jersey

J.G.2 and J.G.53

Portsmouth

Feint against Portsmouth

K.G.54

CHERBOURG 11.00 hrs
(Z.G.26 and Erpr. Gr.210)

LE HAVRE
(Z.G.26)

K.G.55 Form-up Area

Evreux

DREUX
(I/K.G.55)

CHARTRES
(II/K.G.55)

VILLACOUBLAY
(Stab, III/K.G.55)

PARIS

0   50 Miles

Portland, but this order was modified by the Sector Controller who called for the dispatch of two Sections only.

As the German aircraft crossed the coast the fourteen Spitfires of 609 Squadron, led by Squadron Leader Horace Darley, were heading back towards Portland from Swanage, as directed by the Middle Wallop Controller, but no possibility now remained of intercepting the raid before it crossed the coast. The Air Raid Warning Red, the public Alert, had already been issued to coastal areas and now the warning was extended to certain inland areas.

Meanwhile, the two patrolling Spitfires of 152 Squadron's Red Section, at this time over The Needles at 25,000 feet, were ordered to Portland but almost immediately this was changed to proceed to Warmwell to join up with the rest of their squadron then preparing to take-off. No doubt intent on looking for the approaching enemy armada, of which they had been warned, and at the same time following the coastline westwards, the two Spitfire pilots, Flight Lieutenant D.P.A. Boitel-Gill and Pilot Officer R.F. Inness, became separated, but the former caught sight of the enemy as they were crossing the coast. Dismayed but undaunted at the seemingly huge mass of enemy machines, Boitel-Gill manoeuvred into position above and behind them; outnumbered by about 160:1 he wisely decided not to attack but followed the enemy at a discreet distance, hoping to join up with a friendly squadron later on and in the meantime reporting on the Bandits' progress by radio telephone(R/T).

As forecast, the English Channel was cloudless and the Dorset coast was first seen by the German airmen, while some distance away, as a faint smudge in the haze of the horizon, capped by a line of cumulus along its length. As they drew nearer they could make out the unmistakable shape of Portland Bill, with the sweep of Lyme Bay disappearing into the distance on the left and the high cliffs of Lulworth to the right. No better confirmation that they were on track was possible. Surface visibility was not particularly good near the coast, but above the haze layer, from which the tops of the well broken cumulus emerged with a brilliant whiteness, visibility was excellent.

The German formations crossed the coast at 11.23 and were

engaged by Portland's AA batteries, but without effect. From the sling-type seat in the dorsal B-Stand position of his He 111 Georg Engel watched the white smoke puffs of the exploding shells drift back below the trailing edge of the wing. All around him the sky seemed full of He 111s with Bf 110s beyond, all apparently motionless except for a gentle rising and falling movement as their pilots juggled to maintain formation. Facing aft he was more or less looking into the sun, the most likely direction of an enemy attack, but in that direction he could see only friendly aircraft. Engel's He 111 was in the middle of the bomber formation, a position of comparative safety he consoled himself, which also provided them with an excellent view of the entire force. Until recently Engel's attention had been centred upon his FuG X radio equipment, maintaining a listening watch on the *Gruppe* control frequency in case of a recall or any other operational message, but now his eyes were constantly scanning around the sky, above and below the horizon, as he swung his MG 15 machine-gun around on its ring mounting.

Below Engel, sharing the rear crew compartment, Gefreiter Karl Geib stood astride the Bola, manning two MG 15s that were installed one in each side window. As always he carried his good luck talisman, a black cloth doll given him by a girl-friend. Lower still, in the Bola in the floor of the compartment, Unteroffizier Karl Gerdsmeier lay prone, facing aft and also manning an MG 15. All three were wearing lightweight flying suits, parachute harnesses, life jackets, flying boots and flying helmets adorned with oxygen masks and throat microphones. There was little room to spare in the compartment designed originally for two men and now somewhat congested with an additional crew member and extra guns and 7·92 mm machine-gun magazines, but between them the three men covered a good field of view for defensive purposes.

Forward of the aft compartment was the bomb compartment, today containing five SC 250s mounted nose-upwards in cells mounted either side of a narrow walkway that led through another bulkhead into the almost fully glazed nose compartment. Here, seated to the left, Oberleutnant Weigel was fully occupied keeping formation, checking the ground features and monitoring the flight and engine instruments mounted on a panel in the roof. The Plexiglas nose of the He 111 afforded Weigel and his observer, Oberfeldwebel Alfred Narres, an outstanding field of view. Narres had vacated the fold-down seat beside his pilot and now occupied the prone position in the nose; he was normally responsible for the navigation and bomb aiming in addition to manning the A-Stand armament, but on this flight the navigation was the responsibility of the lead observer and bomb release was to be by R/T command. Today, apart from selecting the automatic bomb release sequence on the RAB 14 selector, arming and releasing the bombs, his primary task was to man the MG 15 mounted off-set to starboard in an Icaria cupola mounting in the extreme nose.

Before reaching the English coast engine trouble had forced five more He 111s to abort in addition to Korte's aircraft. All six aircraft – three belonging to Stab/KG 55, two to I Gruppe and the other to II Gruppe – returned safely and were now followed southwards by the Bf 109s that had swept ahead of the main force to circle high over Warmwell before departing for their home bases. They had met no British fighters and returned without having fired their guns in anger.

It soon became apparent that the main force was not engaged in a second phase of an attack on Portland but was continuing inland, a fact confirmed by Observer Corps reports. Meanwhile the Ju 88s of KGs 51 and 54 withdrew on the flanks and the overall picture became clearer, suggesting to the 10 Group controller a penetration by the Heinkels towards Yeovil where the Westland Aircraft factory seemed a likely target. Subsequently 238 Squadron was scrambled from Middle Wallop with instructions to head for a point 10 miles south of Yeovil, climbing to 15,000 feet, but again the order to scramble was much too late.

All other 10 Group fighters already airborne were also ordered to the Somerset town but by now the bombers were only 16 miles from the Westland factory. Upon receipt of these instructions No 609 Squadron, now between Swanage and Portland, and the three Hurricanes of 601 Squadron approaching Portland from the direction of Exeter, turned in pursuit. No contact with the enemy had yet been made by these fighters and only individual pilots of 152 Squadron, taking off singly and in small groups from Warmwell (where, while still on the ground, they had seen the enemy aircraft passing overhead) had the distant enemy in sight.

At 11.28, as Raid 22 approached Yeovil, No 56 Squadron at Boscombe Down was brought to Advanced Readiness, but the enemy by-passed the assumed target and continued towards Weston-super-Mare. At this development 10 Group ordered all available Hurricanes of 79 Squadron at Pembrey to come to Readiness with three Sections to take-off and proceed to Weston as quickly as possible.

Pilot Officer Inness of 152 Squadron, who, it will be recalled, became separated from Derek Boitel-Gill over the Dorset coast, was almost certainly the first British pilot to engage the enemy, and he did so quite alone. Displaying remarkable courage he overtook the enemy bombers and just south of Yeovil turned to carry out a lone head-on attack. As he sliced through the enemy formation he opened fire and broke away downwards, but the combined closing speed of his Spitfire and the He 111s was so great that he was unable to see the results of his attack.

Yellow and White Sections of the same squadron also climbed in pursuit until they were above and in front of the bombers and, again in the vicinity of Yeovil, adopted the same tactics in a combined frontal attack on the enemy's right flank. The four Spitfires then broke formation and climbed back up to continue with individual attacks. Pilot Officer G.J. Cox made a solo head-on attack on one group of German aircraft but his own machine was hit by heavy return fire and he was forced to break off the engagement and return to Warmwell, the action's first known aircraft casualty. His Number Two, Pilot Officer F.H. Holmes, and White Section Leader, Sergeant R. Wolton, made similar attacks but they too failed to see any results. Sergeant J. McBean Christie also attacked a He 111 but blacked-out as he broke away and when he recovered he was unable to re-establish contact with the enemy.

Pilot Officer T.N. Bayles in another Spitfire of the pursuing 152 Squadron had first seen the enemy in the Yeovil area but

Pilot Officer Eric S. Marrs of No. 152 Squadron, RAF.

only managed to catch up with them as they neared Bristol. He then carried out a solo attack but also experienced considerable fire from the German gunners and was unable to observe any positive results. A second attack proved no more successful.

Bayles's Number Two, Pilot Officer Eric S. Marrs, was attacked by some Bf 110s as he made his first attack and he was forced to break away. He afterwards reported that the enemy bombers maintained a good formation for their mutual protection, but he felt that in the main the escort lagged behind the failed to give their charges much protection. Describing his participation in the action in a letter to his father he wrote:

On Wednesday morning a Flight was sent off on patrol. Soon afterwards the rest of the squadron was told to get into the air as quickly as possible. The result was we all went off in bits and pieces. I went off with one other chap and as a pair we went looking for trouble. We climbed to 16,000 feet and saw a tremendous cloud of aircraft just round Yeovil way going north. There were two large groups of bombers consisting of about 40 bombers each. Milling around and above and behind them were numerous 110s acting as guard.

Well, the two of us proceeded north, passed the enemy and came round in front of them. We waited just south of Bristol for them. Then we attacked. We went head-on straight for the middle of the foremost group of bombers. Firing as we went we cut through the heart of them like a knife through cheese; but they wouldn't break. They were good, those Jerry bombers – they stuck like glue. On coming through the first group I ran into some 110s. I milled around with those for a bit trying to get on the tail of one of them, but there was always another to get on my tail. Things became a bit hot, and seeing a 110 very close to getting a lovely shot in on me, I pulled the stick back hard and pushed on full left rudder. I did three smart flick rolls and span. I came out of the spin below everything.

I climbed up to sunwards of everything to have another crack at the bombers, climbing to the same height and slightly in front of them on their starboard side. I saw a Heinkel lagging behind the formation and dived to attack it from the starboard quarter. I got a long burst into it and it streamed glycol from its starboard engine. My attention was then occupied by a 110 which came to the help of the Heinkel. A steep turn was enough to get behind it as it did not seem very anxious to stay and fight. I came in from the starboard quarter again and kept my finger on the firing button, turning in behind it. Its starboard engine (becoming a habit now) streamed glycol.

Suddenly there was an almighty bang and I broke away quickly. I looked around, glanced at my engine and oil tanks and positioned myself for another attack, this time going for the port engine. I just began to fire when my ammunition petered out. I broke away and dived below cloud, throttled back, heaved a deep sigh and looked around to see where I was. I steered south, came to the aerodrome and landed. I had a look at my machine and counted eleven bullet holes in it. The one that made a bang in the cockpit had come along from the rear, nipped in the right hand side of the fuselage and smashed the socket into which the R/T is plugged.

Eric Marrs, nineteen years old and known as 'Boy' to his squadron colleagues, survived the Battle of Britain but was killed in an offensive patrol over Brest in 1941. His letters to his father, written soon after he had been in action, are classics of their kind and reflect the spirit prevailing among the pilots of Fighter Command in 1940.

Almost certainly the lagging He 111 attacked by Marrs was the G1+LR, flown and commanded by the *Staffelkapitän* of the Villacoublay-based 7 Staffel, Oberleutnant Hans Bröcker. With his starboard engine damaged in one of the earliest attacks Bröcker was unable to maintain his position in the formation and to improve the aircraft's performance he decided to jettison his bombs, understandably more concerned with getting back to France than hitting a worthwhile target.

Bristol now appeared to be the most likely objective and accordingly every 10 Group fighter in the air was ordered to this area. They turned in pursuit, at full throttle in response to the command 'Buster', but the late initial orders to take off and their early misdirection made it impossible for them to make an effective interception in strength before the bombers reached their target.

V

Bomben Los!

The people of Bristol continued about their everyday tasks, blissfully unaware of impending events. Since daybreak they had experienced yet another uneventful Alert and there was little reaction when the sirens were heard once more at 11.31. It was Bristol's 168th air raid Alert of the war and, as usual now, scant heed was paid to it. Buses and other traffic continued to move normally although police officers and Air Raid Wardens donned their steel helmets. The city's barrage ballons, glinting silver-grey in the bright sunshine, were already ascending and the gunners of the 76th HAA Regiment, similarly pre-alerted, had taken post and were awaiting developments. In schools throughout the city children filed out of classrooms and made their way to their shelters, rejoicing at the interruption to their lessons, but industry, most commercial undertakings and life in general, went on much as before.

Far to the south, approaching Yeovil from the south-west, the three pilots of 601 Squadron's Red Section saw what they assessed to be 'Eighty Plus Bandits' some distance north. The three Hurricanes gave chase, but it soon became apparent that they were too far behind to catch up. The section leader, Flying Officer H.C. Mayers, reported this by R/T to the sector controller who thereupon instructed the section to proceed to Weston-super-Mare and there await the raiders' return.

Raid 22 reached Weston-super-Mare at 11.38, at precisely which time the three sections of 79 Squadron became airborne from Pembrey with instructions to proceed to a point five miles south of Cardiff, climbing to 15,000 feet. Approaching Weston-super-Mare Major Friedrich Kless ordered his pilot, Oberfeldwebel Jesuiter, to alter course for Filton and the lead aircraft started a slow turn to the right. Kless's G1+AC was followed by the rest of the bombers but not by the fighter escort which maintained its original course. The result was a separation into two distinct formations, giving the impression of a split raid with one part heading for Bristol and the other continuing towards Cardiff. There is no known explanation for this, but possibly the fighter leader failed to notice the bombers' change of course. However, shortly afterwards the Bf 110s turned to follow the bombers, but there was now a gap of about five miles between the two groups.

Upon reaching the Weston-super-Mare turning point the He 111s, hitherto in a fairly open formation, closed up in preparation for bombing, but their groundspeed remained constant throughout at approximately 175 mph. As they approached the south-west outskirts of Bristol a few Spitfires of No 609 Squadron joined those of 152 already in action. Squadron Leader Horace Darley was among the new attackers, intercepting the enemy when they were about three miles from the city. He too noted the bombers' now tight formation and the resultant effective cross-fire from the German gunners, but the Bf 110 fighters were still some three miles distant and appeared to be totally ineffective as an escort.

It was about this time that Sergeant J. Hughes Rees, one of Darley's pilots, carried out an attack on what he mistakenly thought was a Dornier Do 215. Misidentification of Bf 110s, Do 17s and Do 215s was common throughout the Battle of Britain and there is no doubt that the aircraft attacked by Hughes Rees was in fact a Bf 110; he saw the enemy aircraft dive down towards the sea off Portishead, apparently badly damaged, but almost immediately the engine of his Spitfire began to overheat. The oil pressure fell to only 25 pounds and, throttling back, Hughes Rees was forced to glide down to make an emergency landing in a field near Glastonbury Tor, the well known Somerset landmark. He came down about half a mile south of the Tor and escaped injury although the undercarriage of his Spitfire sustained some damage.

By now many Bristolians were aware of a distant pulsating throb. Gradually it swelled to a crescendo of aircraft engine noise, punctuated by bursts of machine-gun fire and the distinctive 'crump' of exploding AA shells as the city's guns opened fire.

Casting his mind back Georg Engel recalls that the first AA bursts were very accurate. He remembers seeing two Spitfires paralleling his formation as they approached the Bristol Channel and he assumed they were relaying details of the Heinkels' height and speed to the ground by R/T. These were the only fighters he had seen until now, but fellow crew member Karl Gerdsmeier remembers seeing about six Spitfires diving headlong through the bombers, pursued by a number of Bf 110s.

At first glance RAF Yatesbury, near Calne in Wiltshire, looked much like any other air force station of the early war years, consisting of a small grass airfield with a hutted camp. Situated on the north side of the main London-Bristol road it was the home of No 2 Radio School. It differed from other stations, however, in having a small compound a mile or so to the east of the main camp, where several unusual wireless masts were to be seen, and it was here that the RAF trained personnel in the operation and maintenance of its highly secret RDF equipment.

In September 1940 Douglas Wingrove was an NCO Instructor at Yatesbury, his particular section dealing with maintenance and fault-finding on CHL (Chain Home, Low) equipment, a radar set designed to detect low flying aircraft at moderate ranges and used in conjunction with the earlier CH Stations. During instructional periods, Wingrove recalls, faults were simulated and rectified, the sets being restored to full working order before the next class period.

On 25th September, with the morning training period completed, a test calibration was arranged, using a light aircraft that was to take off from the adjacent airfield and fly due west. The test calibration began and after the aircraft had been airborne for a few minutes Wingrove noticed what appeared to be a saturation signal on the same bearing but some 35 miles distant on the coast of the Bristol Channel. This was an interesting situation as due to the inland location of the CHL set it should not have been possible to 'see' in this sector because of the intervening high ground. Wingrove's first reaction was to assume a fault in the set, but it soon became apparent that he was, in fact, observing a large number of aircraft flying along the coast of the Bristol Channel and that in all probability they were hostile. The calibration aircraft was advised to return as soon as possible and the Station Commander was informed of the situation. Soon the hut was full of officers and the plotting of the unidentified aircraft continued, those present witnessing, as it later transpired, the attack on Filton and the first known RAF use of an inland radar for tracking enemy aircraft.*

The incident provoked much interest at Fighter Command headquarters and visits by officers from No 10 Group followed. Subsequently it was decided that during non-instructional periods a watch should be maintained and observations fed into the Filter Room at Box for incorporation in the overall plotting system.

After passing Weston-super-Mare, Oberleutnant Weigel informed his crew that he was about to switch the air-to-air R/T communications into the intercom system, at the same time telling them to stop non-essential chatter and listen for any orders from the *Geschwader* leader. These orders were to come from Major Friedrich Kless, who points out that although he was in communication with the bombers he had no R/T contact with the escorting fighters. This, he felt was a great disadvantage.

Gerdsmeier, from his vantage point in the Bola of the G1+DN estimated that the first flak bursts were only some 75 feet below the formation. He then heard the voice of the formation leader in his earphones – '*Das Ziel liegt vor uns!*' – the target lay ahead. Then came instructions from Kless to standby for bombing, followed by an order to the pilots to open formation a little and to reduce height. This last instruction followed the arrival of some more accurately placed AA bursts.

Weigel and Narres in the nose of the G1+DN could clearly see the sun glinting on the tell-tale railway junction and a few moments later they could see the target. Then came the leader's

* At this time only the army possessed radar equipment for inland use, a few short-range sets being in use for gun-laying purposes.

Marksmen. Gunners of 237 Battery, 76th HAA Regiment, responsible for shooting down the He 111 at Failand, 25 September 1940. Kenneth Grater back row, right. Taken at Portbury in May 1941 with a propeller blade from another He 111 shot down in February 1941.

command '*Bombenschächte auf!*' – and in fifty-eight He 111s hands moved in unison to open the bomb doors.

On the Portbury gun-site, near Portishead, the barrels of four 3·7 inch guns swung around to point skywards at the same angle. The layers were obeying the azimuth and elevation pointers controlled by a nearby predictor that was aligned on a selected target aircraft in the middle of the enemy formation, an aircraft leading a 'V' of three machines. In the site Command Post the NCO assistant to the Gun Position Officer was Kenneth Grater, a pre-war Territorial soldier whose home was in Bristol, and as he was responsible for relaying the order to fire he well remembers the events that followed.

The four guns fired simultaneously and almost unbelievably

appeared to score at least one direct hit on their target. The aircraft went into a turn, gradually steepening its angle of bank, but unfortunately the predictor operators continued to follow it, not realising that it was out of control. Accordingly as it spiralled down all predictions for future firing positions were rendered useless – one gun on the site fired another round in desperation, shooting visually 'over the barrel', but the Portbury site was unable to effectively engage the enemy further.

The frustration felt by the Portbury gunners can be imagined; it was ironic indeed that their remarkable shooting resulted in a development that prevented them continuing the action they had started in such a spectacular fashion.

At least one of the shells from the Portbury guns had, in fact, exploded just below the tail of Weigel's aircraft, badly damaging the control surfaces and causing it to go into an uncontrollable turn to the left. Luckily no crew members were injured and the G1+DN did not collide with any other aircraft in the formation. Immediately aware of his machine's lack of controllability Weigel lost no time in ordering his crew to bale out.

Unteroffizier Gerdsmeier climbed up from the Bola at Weigel's command and scrambled through the bomb bay to check on the situation in the nose compartment, but upon reaching the forward bulkhead he found that both Oberleutnant Weigel and Oberfeldwebel Narres were unhurt and were preparing to jump from the emergency exit above the pilot's seat. He then lurched back through the reeling bomb bay to the rear compartment to find Feldwebel Engel and Gefreiter Geib debating whether to go out through the top B-Stand postion or through the hatch in the Bola.

Stooping he quickly opened the latter floor exit, indicating that they should go out that way. Georg Engel climbed down from the B-Stand, gesturing that Gerdsmeier should go first, but as the *Bordmechaniker* was about to step out into space he realised with a start that he had not yet clipped his parachute pack onto his harness. Stepping over the now open hatch to get his pack his left flying boot came off and went out to disappear in the void below. Ignoring his loss he quickly clipped on his parachute, dropped to sit on the edge of the hatchway and, with his feet pressed tightly together, went out with his arms protecting his head.

The first man to get out was Weigel, followed through the front roof exit by Narres. Gerdsmeier was the third to leave, through the Bola, and then came Geib, assisted by a push on the rear from Engel's foot. Engel was by now rather anxious to escape from the crashing Heinkel; his camera, with which he had hoped to obtain some shots of England, was one of the last things he saw as he followed Geib out through the floor of the bomber, but he felt he would have little use for it now.

The G1+DN came spiralling down with increasing speed, its motors overspeeding to a high pitched scream, but it was in a fairly level attitude when it ploughed into a field on Mr Hubert Holder's Racecourse Farm, situated between Portbury and Failand to the west of Bristol. The Heinkel smashed through a hedge into a second field and careered along for a hundred yards or so, breaking up after initial impact and disintegrating as it went. As it first hit the ground its load of five SC 250s were thrown from the shattered bomb bay section of the fuselage, but not being armed they did not explode.

As the dust settled about the scattered wreckage five parachutes appeared in the sky above, with the black dots that were men swinging gently beneath the white canopies as they drifted slowly down over Belmont Hill near Flax Bourton. The time was now 11.45.

The German formation thundered on over Bristol's south-west outskirts, undeterred by the loss of one of their number. So far there had been only limited fighter opposition and the low volume of AA fire, although accurate, was no great deterrent. The absence of heavy gunfire and the apparent absence of RAF fighters led some vociferous citizens to later complain that there had been no opposition at all to the enemy. This allegation, which has been repeated many times, is still widely believed and even a reputable local history* records:

The enemy flew in perfect formation and there were no British

* *Bristol at War* by C.M. MacInnes (Museum Press, London), 1962.

planes to oppose him. He was quite indifferent to the feeble anti-aircraft fire which was all the defenders of the city could do to obstruct his path.

The author concludes:

> No British planes had appeared in the skies of Bristol that morning, and few people paused to ask the reason why. Fortunately no one in the city knew the insignificant number of British fighters which still remained to oppose the enemy.

However, there were indeed fighters in the skies above Bristol that morning, but they were few in number not because of an acute shortage of fighters but because of a general mismanagement of the force available. Further, 'feeble anti-aircraft fire' was not the impression gained by Friedrich Kless, the attack leader, nor by other German airmen who took part, all of whom have stressed the accuracy of the gunfire, the evidence of which was to be found in a field at Failand.

British pilots, too, had cause to complain of the AA fire, for No 609 Squadron Operations Record Book reveals that 'the AA fire over Bristol was disturbing to the pilots, although well meant.' With the overwhelming weight of evidence to the contrary the claim that there was no opposition must be refuted. The truth is there was opposition, but it was limited in extent and was not particularly obvious to observers on the ground.

The cloud cover had gradually increased during the morning, but blue sky was still predominant and the sunlight, reflected upwards from the tops of the brilliant white clouds, highlighted the German aircraft to make them clearly visible from the streets of the city. The spectacle was unequalled by any pre-war air pageant and to the population it seemed quite incomprehensible that the aircraft overhead were German – how could such a possibility be reconciled with the mastery of the air with which the RAF was credited?

Elderly Mrs Annie Tranter's reaction was typical. As she swept the path outside her home her attention was drawn to the approaching bombers by the heavy throb of their engines. A casual discussion with a neighbour led to the mutual conclusion that 'they must be ours, not Jerries', and they started to count what was the biggest group of aircraft they had ever seen. After reaching seventy, however, they gave up.

The engine noise drew hundreds of people from their homes, shops and offices to gaze upwards at the never to be forgotten sight, most of them oblivious of the danger to which they were exposed.

At Filton work in the factories continued normally until the martial strains of 'Marching Through Georgia', the Raid Imminent warning, were heard over the loud-speaker system. At this the employees, including many women, ceased work and made their way to the shelters. This was a fairly common occurrence and one that caused no undue concern; as was usually the case the exodus was accompanied by some good natured banter. It was, after all, a break for many of them from the somewhat monotonous routine of factory work, but as the employees streamed out to the shelters the approaching bombers could be heard and then seen in the distance.

Their bombing run brought KG 55 over all three main factory groups making up the BAC complex. Despite extensive attempts at camouflage by disruptive paintwork the *Geschwader* leader had no difficulty in lining up the formation for the straight run-in required for accurate bombing. Closing formation again, to concentrate the bomb pattern, the pilots carefully maintained station while the observers completed the pre-release drill of selecting and arming the bombs.

At this very moment the twelve Hurricane pilots of No 238 Squadron, haring in from the south-east, saw the enemy aircraft. Climbing strongly they headed for the Bf 110 escort, but coming over the eastern outskirts of Bristol their leader, Squadron Leader Harold Fenton, realised that the bombers were closer and elected to attack them instead. Ordering his pilots into line astern he swung around to attack from above and behind. As he did so Friedrich Kless in the leading bomber, prone over his Lotfe 7C bombsight, released his bombs. At the same time he gave the command '*Bomben los!*' over the R/T.

From the open bellies of fifty-seven He 111s the bombs came

Through the enemy's eyes. These photographs appeared in *Der Adler* magazine and refer to the attack on Filton, 25 September 1940. A translation of the original German caption appears below.

"An Attack and its Results." Our photographs show the large aircraft factories at Filton. The picture on the left was taken a few days before the raid which destroyed the factory. Easily recognised, close to the railway, are the huge workshops whose camouflage was intended to protect them from aerial observation. This air photograph, however, proves that paint on the roof alone is not enough. The workshops are clearly recognisable. The upper picture was taken during the first bombing attack. The main works can be recognised in the left hand lower corner. Bombs are seen exploding in the middle of the works. The somewhat smaller branch factory above the railway which crossed the picture is completely covered by salvoes of bombs. The white patches in the right hand lower corner of the upper picture are clouds which have drifted between the ground and the attacking aircraft. The upper picture enables one to see with all clarity that hell had been let loose on the Filton works below. Blow after blow rains on the great shops. This factory will not produce many more aircraft. The numbers indicate: (1) The main works; (2) Adjoining works; (3) Seven aircraft parked in a line; (4) Three aircraft on the ground; (5) Barrage balloons on the ground; (6) The main runway crossing the middle of the aerodrome.

Ein Angriff und seine Wirkung

Unsere Aufnahmen haben das große Flugzeugwerk von Filton zum Gegenstand. Das Bild links ist wenige Tage vor dem Angriff aufgenommen, der das Werk nahezu vernichtet hat. Deutlich erkennbar sind neben der Bahnlinie die riesigen Werkhallen, deren Tarnbemalung gegen Fliegersicht schützen soll. Das Luftbild beweist aber, daß der Anstrich der Dächer allein nicht genügt. Die Hallen sind vollkommen klar zu erkennen. Das Bild oben ist während des ersten Bombenangriffs aufgenommen. Das Hauptwerk ist in der linken unteren Ecke zu erkennen. Mitten im Werk schlagen Bomben ein. Das etwas kleinere Zweigwerk oberhalb der quer durch das Bild laufenden Bahn ist von Bombensalven vollkommen eingedeckt. Die weißen Stellen in der rechten unteren Ecke des oberen Bildes sind Wolken, die sich zwischen die Erde und die Kampfflugzeuge geschoben haben. Das obere Bild läßt mit aller nur wünschenswerten Deutlichkeit erkennen, daß da unten, im Flugzeugwerk von Filton, die Hölle ist. Einschlag neben Einschlag prasselt in die großen Hallen. Dieses Werk wird nicht mehr viel Flugzeuge herstellen.

Die Zahlen bedeuten (1) das Hauptwerk, (2) das Nebenwerk, (3) sieben aufgestellte Flugzeuge, (4) drei Flugzeuge am Boden, (5) Sperrballone am Boden, (6) die Startbahn, die mitten durch den Flugplatz führt

Aufnahmen Luftwaffe (2)

tumbling out, turning over as they fell from their vertical nose-upwards stowage to disappear against the background of houses, streets, parks and factories 15,000 feet below. There followed the most devastating bombing yet experienced in the area, the concentration being mainly in a box measuring about one mile wide and three-quarters of a mile deep. Some 350 bombs cascaded down onto this area, in the centre of which lay the Filton factories, in an almost classical 'pattern' or 'carpet' bombing attack. It was precisely 11.48.

Good fortune again favoured the attackers – to have got so far for the loss of only one aircraft was remarkable enough, and their luck held during the final part of the bombing run as a large patch of cloud moved in over the target from the west. It was a race against time which the leading bombers narrowly won, for at the moment of bomb release Filton aerodrome was slowly disappearing from sight. Only the factories on the eastern boundary were visible; moments later and they, too, would have disappeared from view, but they remained in sight long enough for the German crews to see the results of their bombing.

The two crews of Stab/KG 55 later reported that their bombs (eight SC 250s) had landed on the western end of the aero-engine works. The same part of the target was claimed to have been hit by the eighteen crews of I Gruppe, who dropped sixty-eight SC 250s and seventeen delayed action SC 250 LZZs. The twenty He 111s of II Gruppe dropped 150 SC 250s, nine SC 250 LZZs, and four SC 50s, their crews claiming fifteen direct hits on five buildings with further strikes on the north and south sides of the main engine works and on the aircraft factory. More bombs were seen to fall between the factory and the engine test beds and on the nearby railway junction. The seventeen crews of III Gruppe claimed between ten and twelve direct hits on the assembly buildings in the east part of the aircraft factory with more hits on the railway fork to the west of the works and on the south-east corner of the airfield. They dropped seventy-four SC 250s and twenty-four Flam C 250 oil-filled incendiary bombs.

From 15,000 feet the entire target area appeared to be well and truly covered by the rippling flashes of the many bombs exploding almost simultaneously, and dense smoke followed as fires resulted. There was a feeling of exultation among many participating German crew members; their task had been completed as ordered, and they had every reason to feel well satisfied with events so far. They now had only to get home safely.

VI

War over Wessex

The German formation maintained its course for a short while after bombing and then started a slow turn to the right. As it did so Squadron Leader Fenton's twelve Hurricanes came hurtling down, diving from 22,000 feet in line astern. They passed through the middle of the He 111s firing as they went and zoomed back up in climbing turns to continue with individual attacks which they maintained until the raiders recrossed the South Coast.

The fierce combats now developing involved both He 111s and Bf 110s. The latter adopted their usual tactics of forming defensive circles, making elongated circuits with a long run towards the south-east, and continuing to show a reluctance to break out and engage the Hurricanes and Spitfires that were attacking the bombers lower down.

Squadron Leader Peter Devitt, leading four Spitfires of 152 Squadron, caught up with the enemy shortly before they reached Bath. Ordering a Number One Attack the Spitfires went in against three He 111s on the enemy's right flank. Devitt opened fire and saw tracer and incendiary bullets going into the centre-section of a Heinkel as he closed to twenty yards, but then return fire penetrated the fuel tank mounted in front of his cockpit. Fortunately the tank did not explode or catch fire, but petrol sprayed back over Devitt's windscreen, blinding him and forcing him to break off the action. Spiralling down he made a wheels-up forced landing in a field near Skew Bridge at Newton St Loe, three miles west of Bath.

The deadly cross-fire from the bombers provided them with a good measure of protection and their crews realised the importance of staying with the formation – they knew only too well that to lag behind was to court disaster for deprived of mutual defensive fire no single bomber could hope to survive against the eight-gun British fighters. Nevertheless, several German bombers, damaged in varying degrees began to slow down and thereby opened out the previously tight formation.

One damaged He 111 that began to straggle at this point was the G1+BH of 1 Staffel, based at Dreux and commanded by Hauptmann Karl Köthke who, on this occasion, was leading the *Staffel* in the absence of Hauptmann Rudolf Kiel. All had gone seemingly well until leaving the target area when the starboard engine caught fire. Feldwebel Fritz Jürges, Köthke's pilot, carried out the feathering drill and brought the fire under control, but the Heinkel was unable to maintain speed on one engine. The crew could not be certain when or where they had been hit, but even before reaching Filton they had been attacked by Spitfires, one passing within about sixty feet of the German aircraft and giving the acting *Staffel* leader a clear view of its pilot.

Although aware of the seriousness of their position, Köthke made light of it to his crew, reminding them that many German aircraft in a similar predicament had managed to get back to France on one engine. With luck there was no reason why they should not succeed, too. But even as he spoke they slowly dropped back out of position, gradually losing both height and speed despite all the efforts of Fritz Jürges at the controls.

Pilot Officer Dudley Williams, a Section Leader in 152 Squadron, was in no mood to wait for stragglers but went straight for the leader of a 'V' of three He 111s now at 16,000 feet over Bath. Both engines of the bomber streamed smoke as it banked away out of formation, clearly badly damaged. Williams broke away and watched the Heinkel curve away downwards against a patchwork background of fields and cumulus clouds. As it went down he saw it being attacked by other fighters, but the British pilot's attention was then drawn to the Bf 110s which at last began to intervene in some numbers.

The He 111 damaged by Dudley Williams (who marred his performance only by wrongly identifying it as a Ju 88) was the G1+EP flown by the *Staffelkapitän* of 6 Staffel, Hauptmann Helmut Brandt. The Heinkel was shattered by a hail of bullets and was doomed from the start, but it was nevertheless attacked by four more fighters before it finally came to grief. One of its assailants was Sergeant R. Little of 238 Squadron who, after engaging a 110 in combat, without apparent effect, found himself in close proximity to a He 111 and being in a favourable firing position gave it a one second burst with his eight Brownings from 100 yards range. He broke away and then repeated the attack, whereupon black objects were seen to come away from the Heinkel's port engine.

Two Spitfires then joined in the affair and Little watched the enemy machine steepen its dive, momentarily level off and then continue down to crash into a field, exploding and catching fire as it struck the ground. Circling around the crashed bomber Sergeant Little saw one of the attacking Spitfires also crash in an adjacent field and noticed a parachute drifting to the ground nearby.

Brandt's He 111 was also partly shared by Pilot Officer T.N. Bayles of 152 Squadron who had previously attacked a 'Vic' of three aircraft in the main formation. After carrying out a beam attack he looked back to see only two machines where previously there had been three. He also saw a parachute blossom out, but his attention was then drawn to a He 111 diving towards the clouds below – Brandt's aircraft – and he gave chase, attacking it from above and behind. Bayles then found that he was in the company of another Spitfire and two Hurricanes, all of which were trying to get in 'squirts' at the German bomber, which was now down to a very low height. At this point, much too late for safety, two crew members baled out and shortly afterwards the Heinkel hit the ground.

Mr Thomas Meadway was a witness to the last moments of the He 111. He saw the bomber being attacked by the fighters as, with cartridge cases showering down onto the road beside him, the aircraft passed low overhead. The bomber was trailing smoke as the two crew members tried to bale out, but with their parachutes only partly opened, they were killed when they landed about 400 yards away on the outskirts of the village of Woolverton.

The aircraft appeared to crash in the direction of Meadway's home and he set off in that direction with all haste, concerned for the safety of his family. His fears were groundless, however, for the rising pall of smoke led him to a field near Church Farm, close to the picturesque little church at Woolverton. Burning wreckage was spread over an area of some fifty yards square, but no damage was done to any farm property.

In the next field more local residents arrived at the site of the crashed Spitfire to find its pilot, Sergeant K.C. Holland, dead in the cockpit. Kenneth Holland, a young Australian who had been flying as Blue Two to Squadron Leader Devitt, had almost certainly been hit by return fire from the Heinkel's gunners shortly before they crashed. Later a memorial stone was erected on the spot where Holland, known also as Kenneth Holland Ripley, was killed, placed there by his step-father, himself a serving officer in the Royal Air Force.

Following the loss of Brandt's Heinkel the lead of 6 Staffel was assumed by the G1+AP commanded by Oberleutnant Helmut Kindor, but this aircraft too was shortly to be damaged by British fighters.

By now 'A' Flight of No 56 Squadron had been scrambled from Boscombe Down, becoming airborne as the returning enemy aircraft were approaching Sturminster Newton, but the delay in ordering this squadron into the air resulted in it taking no part in the action.

As the Bf 110s of ZG 26 attempted to ward off the British fighters they were themselves attacked. Dudley Williams of 152 Squadron, with Brandt's He 111 already largely to his credit, rejoined the mêlée with an attack on one of the German fighters, in the course of which he was joined by a Hurricane of 601 Squadron. The unfortunate German aircraft proved to be an aircraft of 8/ZG 26 flown by Feldwebel Walter Scherer and crewed by wireless operator/gunner Gefreiter Heinz Schumacher. Scherer was one of the Horst Wessel Geschwader's more successful pilots, credited with ten victories over Allied aircraft, but he had no chance when simultaneously attacked by the two British aircraft. He was at 19,000 feet at the time and the attack, coming from out of the sun, took the German crew unawares. Bullets thudded into their aircraft, wounding Scherer and almost certainly killing his crewman. The Bf 110's port

Feldwebel Walter Scherer (right), a Bf 110 pilot with ZG 26, with his chief mechanic or Crew Chief, Oberwerkmeister Baron. Scherer was shot down over Wiltshire following the attack on Filton.

engine caught fire and almost immediately Scherer lost consciousness as two bullets grazed his skull. The German pilot had flown a wide variety of aircraft since joining the Luftwaffe in 1935, ranging from the Ju 52 transport to the Bf 109, and his experience stood him in good stead when he regained consciousness to find himself only a few hundred feet above the ground. Blood from his head wounds badly obscured his vision but he instinctively switched off both engines, regained control of his aircraft and brought it down in a brilliantly executed belly landing on a hillside at Well Bottom, alongside Greatridge Wood, some 2½ miles south-west of Boyton, Wiltshire.

As the German aircraft retreated south-eastwards over the rolling green and gold-tinted autumn landscape of the West Country, the three Hurricanes of 601 Squadron, circling over Weston-super-Mare to await the return of the enemy set course to intercept the raiders they had previously been unable to catch. Led by Flying Officer H.C. Mayers the three Hurricanes caught up with the enemy near Frome and immediately carried out a frontal attack from out of the sun onto a group of fifteen or so Bf 110s. They were joined, as already described, by the Spitfire of Dudley Williams and one of the German fighters, now known to have been Walter Scherer's aircraft, was seen to trail smoke from both engines. The Hurricanes climbed back up to continue with individual attacks and Mayers and his two colleagues, Flying Officer J.S. Jankiewicz, an exiled Pole, and Pilot Officer A.J.H. Aldwinkle, subsequently claimed two Bf 110s destroyed and one damaged for no loss or damage to themselves.

In the course of the engagement individual combats did not go entirely in favour of the RAF, as might be expected. In one fighter-versus-fighter action a Hurricane of No 238 Squadron was damaged and finally wrecked when making a forced landing at Charmy Down, near Bath. Its pilot, Sergeant F.A. Sibley, was unhurt, as was another pilot of the same squadron, Pilot Officer D.S. Harrison, who made a forced landing with a bullet through his Hurricane's radiator. Harrison made a good landing in a field near Mells Road Railway Station, between Frome and Radstock, and later took-off again, arriving back at Middle Wallop at 14.20 hours.

The last moments of Hans Bröckers He 111, G1+LR, low over the rooftops at Poole.

The Spitfires of 152 Squadron, some of which had been among the first British fighters to engage the enemy, continued their attacks until the German formation crossed the Hampshire coast, and it was here that Derek Boitel-Gill, who had shadowed the enemy all the way from Portland on their inward flight, decided to carry out a frontal attack on what he and a lot more British pilots thought were Ju 88s. After his attack Boitel-Gill saw that one German aircraft was trailing smoke as it dived towards a layer of cloud below. Following it down he found himself over the sea off Swanage, at which point the enemy aircraft disappeared below cloud.

As the He 111s of KG 55 approached Bournemouth, by which time the Bf 109s detailed to cover their withdrawal were approaching from the south, three He 111s in a loose 'V' lagging behind the main force were attacked by Pilot Officers R.F.G. Miller and N. le C. Agazarian of No 609 Squadron. Immediately

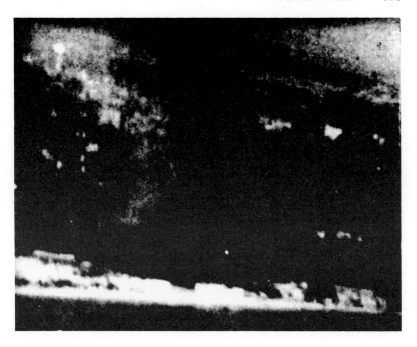

A camera gun shot of the crash of G1+LR at Branksome Park, Poole.

two of the three Heinkels dived for the protection of the clouds below. One was then pursued by Pilot Officer J.R. Urwin-Mann in a Hurricane of 238 Squadron and after a two-seconds burst of fire from seventy yards one of the Heinkel's crew was seen to bale out. With its port engine on fire the bomber steepened its dive towards the coast where it levelled out. Firing another burst Urwin-Mann saw another two men bale out from a height of about 1,000 feet. Both alighted in the sea, a short distance from the shore, but before they reached the water their aircraft hit the ground, crashing into a clifftop house at Branksome Park, Poole, and bursting into flames.

People living in Poole saw three objects appear from the bomber as it passed low overhead, on fire, and shortly afterwards three parachutes were seen to open. Another similar object, now recognised as a man baling out, was seen to turn over and over as it fell, but no parachute opened this time. Shortly afterwards, at 12.09 and still being followed by Urwin-Mann's Hurricane and the Spitfires of Miller and Agazarian, the Heinkel crashed in the select residential area. It demolished a stone wall before striking the side of a large house in Westminster Road, erupting into a mass of flames with its pilot still inside. The Heinkel, which was in fact Hans Bröcker's G1+LR, damaged by Eric Marrs before it reached Bristol and consequently unable to keep up with the formation, was totally destroyed and burning petrol from its ruptured tanks cascaded over the house, the garden and adjacent trees, starting fires but injuring none of the residents.

The second He 111 seen to be in trouble as it passed over the Bournemouth area was the G1+BH of 1/KG 55, flown by Feldwebel Fritz Jürges. Damaged and, it will be recalled, flying on one engine since attacked by fighters over Bath, the G1+BH stood little chance of reaching France, despite the encouraging remarks of the aircraft's *Kommandant*, Hauptmann Karl Köthke. Continuing his account of that day the German officer recalled:

> As we continued on one motor we were left behind and as the Messerschmitt 110 escort did not stay with us we just had to carry on alone. We then lost height rapidly – our aim now was to reach a point in mid-Channel where our air/sea rescue ships were standing-by for such eventualities. As bad luck would have it we passed over an airfield from which we could see fighters taking off, leaving clouds of dust behind them, and we knew the end must come for us soon. We tried in the end to dive for cloud cover, but the clouds were insufficient for our purpose and at a height of about 6,000 feet we were again attacked by fighters. With our few machine-guns we stood no chance. Josef Altrichter, our flight mechanic, was badly wounded in his right leg and as he wore flying overalls we were unable to apply a tourniquet. We knew we could not save him.
>
> We were then hit in our left engine, which stopped as we crossed the English coast. All hopes of reaching mid-Channel now disappeared. We turned in over the coast at a height of about 1,000 feet to attempt a landing and although the

fighters were still following us they did not shoot any more. They knew we could not escape. We lost height very quickly now, heading straight for a quarry, but at the very last moment we managed to gain a little height and found ourselves over fields heading towards a small wood. We touched down and after sliding a short distance came to a standstill, a tree stopping us short.

Köthke's aircraft was finally brought down by the efforts of Pilot Officer J.S. Wigglesworth in a Hurricane of No 238 Squadron. Clearly badly damaged and with its undercarriage hanging down as a result of a wrecked hydraulic system, the He 111 crash landed in a mangold field near Studland. The unlocked undercarriage collapsed on touch-down and in a cloud of swirling dust and flying earth the Heinkel skidded along on its belly and practically severed a wing when it struck a pole carrying an overhead power cable. Circling low over the crashed aircraft Wigglesworth saw three crew members climb out, pulling two others with them. He then left the scene, landing at Warmwell to refuel before returning to Middle Wallop.

And so the German aircraft continued out over the coast and across the English Channel towards France and safety, but the parting shots of the coastal AA guns were not the end of the battle. A damaged Bf 110 of III/ZG 26 was to meet its end in the English Channel, but before ditching its crew managed to transmit a message enlisting the aid of the Seenotdienst, the GAF's Rescue Service. They were later picked up uninjured. Another damaged aircraft, a He 111 of II/KG 55, struggled back to make a crash landing at Caen with two wounded crew members on board. This aircraft, which was a 50% write-off, was the G1+AP commanded by Oberleutnant Kindor, the officer who took over the lead of 6 Staffel when Hauptmann Brandt was shot down at Woolverton. Kindor was badly wounded and for his performance on this mission and seven previous war flights he was highly commended by his *Gruppenkommandeur*.

There were other narrow escapes. Oberleutnant Werner Oberländer and his crew were particularly fortunate when they were attacked by fighters shortly after dropping their bombs.

Villacoublay, where KG 55's *Stabstaffel* and III Gruppe were based.

Their Heinkel was heavily hit by machine-gun fire but no one was wounded. No serious damage was apparent and only when they reached Villacoublay and prepared to land was it realised that the Heinkel's hydraulic system had been hit. Upon selecting the undercarriage down all system pressure was lost and the floor of the Bola became flooded with hydraulic fluid. Using the emergency hand-pump Oberländer's flight mechanic managed to get the undercarriage down but it was then discovered that one tyre had been damaged by machine-gun fire. In spite of these difficulties Oberländer made a successful landing, carefully touching down on one wheel and holding the other off the ground for as long as possible. Examination of the aircraft later revealed no less than 152 bullet holes, a remarkable illustration of the He 111's ability to absorb battle damage.

More He 111s were slightly damaged but total figures are not available. However, Martin Reiser recalls that several aircraft of his *Staffel* were hit by flak or fighters, his own G1+FT receiving two bullets. In exchange twelve machine-gun magazines (900 rounds) were expended by his crew against British fighters.

Several Bf 110s of ZG 26 were also damaged with two in serious trouble on their return flight, but they managed to reach France; one was assessed to be a 60% write-off when it crash-landed at Theville but the other was only slightly damaged. The crews of both escaped unharmed.

In return for what had apparently been achieved at Filton the German casualties – five missing, two badly damaged and a number slightly damaged – were considered acceptable, according the Friedrich Kless, and this is supported by the fact that the very next day two *Gruppen* of KG 55 carried out a similar attack on the Supermarine factory at Woolston. This also achieved good results, but to the Filton raid, despite its mauling on the return flight, must go the distinction of being the more successful. Indeed it was probably the most successful attack against an aircraft factory in the entire Battle of Britain.

IN MEMORY OF EMPLOYEES
KILLED IN AN AIR RAID ON THE COMPANY'S WORKS SEPTEMBER 1940.

ALEXANDER, F.	COOK, Joan L.	LEY, E. E.	SKIPPON, H.
ANDERSON, B. V.	COURT, L. G.	LUCK, E.	SMITH, S.D.C.
ASH, E. W.	EAST, F. E.	MANLEY, T.	SQUIRE, A. M.
ASHMEAD, R. E.	EXTON, J. A.	MULLENS, E. B.	STAPPON, Minnie M.E.
ASPINALL, G. R.	FISHER, A. E.	MYERS, Eliza.	STEPHENS, T.
BABER, A. S.	FORD, J.	NOTTON, R. T.	STEPHENS, W. L.
BAILEY, A.	GRANT, G. B.	OLLIS, W. S.	STRADLING, W. T.
BARNETT, Mabel.	GREEN, G.	OWENS, E.	TAYLOR, E. E.
BAYFORD, D. H.	GREEN, G. E.	OXLEY, R. S.	TUTCHER, E. E.
BAYNTUM, J.	HAINES, F. H.	PACKER, F. W. E.	VICKERY, Barbara J.
BIRD, G.	HARRIS, S.	PARRY, J.	WALKER, A. E.
BISHOP, G.	HEK, P. G.	PLUNKETT, A. G. W.	WARING, Ivor A.
BONE, R.	HILL, G. F. E.	PREWETT, M.G.	WASHINGTON, A.
BOULTER, J.	HOBBS, Maud E. M.	PUGH, T. S.	WATKINS, A. J.
BOYCE, R. C.	HOLLISTER, W. C.	RATCHFORD, J.	WEBB, S. J.
BRITTON, Florence N.	HOLLOWAY, F. W.	REES, T. H.	WEBB, W. H.
BROWN-COLE, G.	HOPTON, Elsie M.	RHYMES, F. J. L.	WELLS, Muriel B.
BURT, E. W.	HORNSBY, S. G.	ROBERTS, V. L.	WESLAKE, Margaret E.
CHENOWETH, Winifred M.	HOYLE, G. E.	ROSSITER, W. A.	WHITE, C.
COATS, Rosemary E.	JONES, G.	SCOTT, Rosemary K.	WHITE, J. T.
COLES, Pamela W.	LANGDON, G. E.	SHORT, E.	WOOD, G. C.
COLSTON, E. W.	LATHAM, Kathleen D.	SHORTMAN, G. T.	YOUNG, E.G.
COOK, D. A. W.	LEWIS, H.	SILCOCK, J.	

ROLL OF HONOUR.
The brass plaque in the entrance hall of Filton House, the former Head Office of The Bristol Aeroplane Company. Unveiled and dedicated by the Lord Bishop of Bristol, it lists employees killed in the attack of 25th September 1940.

VII

The Stricken Factory

The reports received from the returning crews of KG 55 left the Staff Officers of Luftflotte 3 in no doubt whatsoever that the attack had been a resounding success and it was confidently assumed that at least a large part of the Filton complex had been destroyed. There was every reason to believe that production would be gravely affected if not totally halted, but the German Air Force was guilty of over-estimating its success. Sub-contracting to many local firms, large and small, had widely dispersed the production of Bristol aircraft and engines and although the damage inflicted had been extremely serious it was not crippling.

As the employees of the Bristol Aeroplane Company made their way to the air raid shelters Mr Glyn Jones of the works' Air Raid Precautions Advisory Board was standing on top of a shelter near Filton House, on the hill overlooking the airfield and the factories, and he had a remarkable view of the bombing. The first bombs appeared to fall on the Rodney Works, just down the hill from Filton House (the Company's head-office building), and as the dust, smoke and debris shot up more bombs came cascading down, falling all over the factory area.

Some workers had barely reached the shelters before the first bombs arrived and within fifteen to twenty seconds it was all over. Many of the bombs, which fell short of, upon and beyond the target to a depth of three-quarters of a mile, landed on the airfield and on nearby residential areas, while others, possibly due to 'hang-ups' or premature release, fell some miles away in various parts of Somerset and Gloucestershire. In Somerset bombs were reported at Nailsea, Wakendean Siding near Yatton, Abbots Leigh, Failand, Chelvey, Tyntesfield, Standford and Somerset Ashcott. At Stoke-under-Ham, in the same county, a man died from injuries caused by machine-gun fire as the battle raged overhead. In Gloucestershire bombs fell at Stoke Gifford and Winterbourne while in Wiltshire another person, this time a woman, was injured by machine-gun fire.

Altogether more than 900 houses in the Filton area were damaged or destroyed. The mainline railway between Filton Junction and Patchway was blocked and at North Filton both 'up' and 'down' lines were hit. At Filton village and at nearby Westbury-on-Trym bombs damaged water mains besides disrupting gas, electricity and telephone services. Damage to houses in these districts led to the evacuation of some four hundred people, many of whom were accommodated in five hostels previously prepared for such an eventuality. Unexploded bombs brought their share of problems, too, and led to evacuations, road closures and numerous traffic diversions. Damage was also reported in the Southmead district, but it was within the confines of the premises of the Bristol Aeroplane Company that most damage was done and where the greatest number of casualties occurred.

There is some doubt about the precise number of casualties as those within the works perimeter are not included in the official Bristol casualty list, but it appears that outside the factory fifty-eight people were killed, 154 seriously injured and 118 slightly hurt. It was also reported that eleven soldiers were killed as they marched along the road between the Rodney Works and Patchway. Within the factory area it is believed that 72 were killed and 166 injured, of which number 19 later died from their injuries.

The high death roll among BAC employees was mainly caused by a series of direct hits by high-explosive bombs on six crowded air raid shelters, and upon arrival rescue and first aid personnel were confronted with terrible scenes. Some shelters had caved in, burying their occupants, while others were blasted wide open, the craters revealing bodies mutilated and dismembered by the violence of the explosions. Distinguishing the dead from the dying or badly injured was a task not readily forgotten by those to whom this duty fell.

There were countless examples of bravery among those at the

receiving end of the bombing that day, but few endured more than fifty-year-old Mrs Alice Peacock. Shortly after the factory warning she was sitting in No 1 Shelter with some friends, most of whom were talking or knitting, when there was a tremendous explosion. Mrs Peacock was found some distance away, covered by debris and trapped by her legs, but still conscious. About three hours later, during which time she was given pain relieving drugs, she was released and taken to hospital in Bristol with many other injured BAC employees.

Alice Peacock was not traced by her family until mid-afternoon of the next day, when they discovered that she was alive but had lost both legs. She eventually mastered the use of artificial limbs and returned to her home in Bishopston. When fully recovered she resumed her war work at Filton, an unsung heroine surely deserving of recognition. And she was by no means alone in her courage and steadfastness.

The large number of people killed and injured made notification of next-of-kin and the identification of bodies very difficult. Filton Church was pressed into use as a temporary mortuary and an excellent job was done by company welfare officers and others who made innumerable visits to bereaved relatives and others. Apart from the personal tragedies the war effort also suffered for among those killed were valuable technical staff who proved difficult to replace in a highly specialised industry.

While works' firemen strove to extinguish the fires that resulted, assistance was rushed to Filton by the Bristol ARP and the Fire Services and scenes of sheer chaos greeted them upon arrival. Buildings and vehicles burned furiously in a smoke-filled, dust-laden atmosphere while stunned survivors, many of whom had miraculous escapes from death or serious injury, made their way over rubble-strewn roads within the factory complex. Rescue attempts were seriously hampered by a large number of delayed action or 'dud' bombs that were scattered far and wide; of twenty ambulances sent to Filton seven were damaged by bombs which exploded after the attack. The delayed action bombs also caused nine casualties among first aid and medical personnel.

Bomb damage. This reconnaissance photo of Filton was taken on 27th September 1940 by a Ju 88 of 2(F)/123 flown by Feldwebel August Herbst. Despite camouflage attempts, the engine works at Patchway are readily discernible to the right of Filton's east-west runway, shown here under construction. The main landing area is broken up by cinders to resemble a typical field patchwork. The railway pattern to the right of the complex makes the attempts at camouflage almost superfluous.

Secret Fighter. A Beaufighter Mk I night fighter at Filton. This type was still on the Secret List at the time of the attack on Filton, 25th September 1940. The houses in the left distance mark the northern boundary of the airfield.

Damage to RAF premises on the north side of the airfield was minimal, but the disruption of telephone communications between the Filton Sector Operations Room and No 10 Group Headquarters was a serious matter.

As reported by the German crews, most of the ninety tons of high explosives and all 24 oil bombs landed on or around the target. In total 168 bombs were counted within the factory area, extensively damaging the Rodney Works and causing many casualties at the Flight Shed and East Engine Works, where the six shelters were hit. The main aircraft assembly halls were hit and severely damaged and two of the five buildings concerned with engine manufacture were damaged; one building was almost totally destroyed by fire and the roof of another was shattered. Eight newly-built aircraft were destroyed and another twenty-four were damaged. Machine tools suffered badly, both by bombing and by the effects of water when some mains were fractured, and further water damage was caused by the factory sprinkler system. In the factory car parks numerous vehicles were damaged and many were burnt out.

Nevertheless, serious though the damage was – and

production was affected for some time – the factory was far from being totally destroyed. It took several months to get back to normal levels of production, as a study of Beaufighter production* reveals, but the prior dispersal and sub-contracting policy helped enormously to minimise the effect of the attack.

Efforts to make good the damage at Filton and at the Rodney Works and Patchway met with a degree of success that exceeded all expectations. The speed with which electric power was restored, for example, was typical, the current being reinstated within five hours. This was a magnificent effort that was justly applauded by Lord Beaverbrook, the Minister for Aircraft Production, when he visited the factory a few days later.

One effect of the raid that the Germans could not determine was the remarkable change it produced upon the civilian population. Until now, with bombing of a generally desultory nature, few people seemed to have feelings against Germany that could be termed close to hatred but now, with many homes in and around Bristol mourning the loss of relatives and friends, feelings hardened. Despite the generally acknowledged legitimacy of the target there was a new loathing of the Nazis, as all Germans were then termed, and especially of 'Nazi airmen'. This strengthened still further the determination to resist the enemy, no matter what, and indirectly fortified the civil population against heavier and much more destructive attacks that were yet to come. But all of this was in the future and it was the present that occupied the thoughts of the people at Filton when, at 12.16, the sirens sounded the long, steady note of the All Clear, for although the raiders had departed, the task of retrieving the bodies of the dead and tending the wounds of the injured was just beginning.

Rescue work and the clearing of roads blocked by rubble had barely got under way when, about an hour after the All Clear, the sirens again brought work to a halt. This time, however, the intruder was only a high flying enemy reconnaissance aircraft bent on photographing the results of the attack.

* No Beaufighters were produced during the weeks ending 28th September and 5th October. Figures for the following three weeks were four, six and nine aircraft.

Throughout the rest of the day, and for much of the next, explosions continued to rock the Filton district as delayed action bombs detonated. Word of the disaster at the factory spread throughout Bristol and its environs and the homecoming of employees was awaited with trepidation. In many cases the fears were groundless but for others the previously distant horrors of total warfare became a close and tragic reality.

VIII

Unwelcome Guests – 1

The German aircraft brought down over the West Country and the South of England brought much drama and excitement to several normally quiet districts where little ever seemed to happen to disturb the tranquillity of rural life. The first people at the scene of the crashes were usually local residents, some of whom were invariably members of the Home Guard, but the police or military personnel were always quick to arrive to keep sightseers and souvenir hunters at bay.

The population derived great pleasure from the sight of a crashed German aircraft and there was also an element of curiosity about its crew. International travel was not the commonplace event it is today and few country people in those days had ever seen a German before, apart from ex-Servicemen who had served in France in the Great War. The Englishman's inherent suspicion of foreigners was probably at its zenith in 1940 and to many people, and not only country folk, the Germans were more like aliens from another planet than mortal beings from a nearby Continental country. The British reacted to them in a variety of ways; hatred, fear, indifference, friendliness, and compassion were all to be seen, but at first most people undoubtedly had certain misgivings at finding themselves in the presence of members of the German armed forces.

The German airmen, too, had misgivings as they descended into the abode of an enemy they had been attacking. Certainly the crew of Oberleutnant Weigel's Heinkel had misgivings as they drifted down over Belmont Hill, just to the west of Bristol. All five men descended in close proximity and looking around they could see each other and some barrage balloons which at one time looked disconcertingly close. They could also see the aircraft of their comrades – from whom they were now irrevocably separated – approaching Filton and after a while could see the bombs erupting over the target area and the rising pall of smoke. Below them they had already seen their 'Dora Nordpol' spiral down to crash on farmland.

As Karl Gerdsmeier seemingly slowly came down his thoughts turned to his packed bags back at Chartres airfield, all ready for his departure on leave. His mind was in something of a turmoil, but the seriousness of his position was clear – down below was England; what was he to expect, where would he land and what would happen to him? Recalling that traumatic moment Gerdsmeier said:

> I saw some people running over the meadows in my direction and as I came nearer to the ground I could see that they were wearing steel helmets and carrying sticks, pitchforks and guns. 'Home Guard' were the words that immediately came to mind. Suddenly the ground came up, quicker than I expected, and I landed heavily, badly hurting my left knee and falling onto my back. The breath was knocked from my body and I had a severe pain in my leg. I was still unable to breathe properly when the men arrived to find me lying on my back. They lifted me to my feet and one of them thrust the muzzle of a gun in front of my face. I was still fighting for breath and quite unable to move, but looking beyond my captors I saw a car come to a stop on a road about 400 yards away and a policeman got out. As I was unable to move my arms I could not release my parachute harness, nor could I reach my pistol. Kicks and blows then rained down on me and I was struck with the butt of a gun. I fell to the ground, only to be lifted again and my watch and a ring on my finger forcibly removed. The policeman, now hurrying across the field, called in a loud voice and the men released me. Upon reaching us he lifted my arms, enabling me to breathe, and asked if I spoke English and whether or not I was injured. I replied 'Only a little' to both questions. Looking back I feel certain that my life was saved by that policeman.

It is doubtful if Gerdsmeier's life was actually in danger, but it seems likely that he would have received even rougher treatment from his captors but for the presence of the late Sergeant Dix of the Long Ashton police. The police sergeant assisted the German airman across the field to his car but shrugged his shoulders when Gerdsmeier tried to indicate that his watch and ring had been taken. They then drove to Flax Bourton Police Station and on the way the Sergeant gave Gerdsmeier a cigarette. 'It was a Woodbine', the airman recalled, 'the sweetest cigarette of my life'.

Gerdsmeier is, to this day, full of praise for Sergeant Dix. He decided, as they drove along, that he was 'a fine gentleman, as one expected of an Englishman;' the others, he felt, 'had been influenced by hysterical propaganda and were not really responsible for their actions'. Besides taking his watch and ring they had also removed his Luger P 08 pistol, had unzipped his flying suit and emptied his pockets. They also attempted to remove the Iron Cross from the lower left breast position of his flight blouse. This last move the German tried to resist, so far as he was able, and it was this that brought on the blows.

Georg Engel, the wireless operator, was also somewhat apprehensive of his reception when shortly before he landed he too saw four or five men of the Home Guard running towards his probable landing place. Also landing heavily Engel rolled over in agony as an intense pain shot through his right leg.

First to reach him was Mr C.B. Ball who was working in a small hut at Failand when he heard the sound of the crashing aircraft. Ball, 'Chubby' to his Home Guard colleagues, saw the parachutist coming down and grabbing his .22 rifle set off in pursuit. After running about a mile he came across the German airman laying on the ground and saw at once that he had a broken leg. More men soon arrived on the scene and they removed his P 08 pistol and aircrew knife, emptied his pockets of cigarettes, sweets and a pocket knife, but allowed him to retain some family snapshots, a concession for which Engel was very grateful. Two sticks were applied to his leg as temporary splints and before long an ambulance and a police officer arrived, summoned by the local Home Guard Battalion HQ.

Feldwebel Engel had landed near Charlton House, on the

Sailard Road, and from here he was taken to Clevedon Cottage Hospital where he was placed in a small ward beside a wounded British soldier. He remembers with gratitude that he was fairly treated by the hospital staff and the next day he unexpectedly received some cigarettes, fruit and chocolate from an army sergeant and another soldier who were visiting their wounded colleague in the next bed.

In retrospect Karl Geib now considers the 25th September to have been his lucky day for he survived the war whereas many of his comrades in KG 55 were to lose their lives either over England or, later on, in Russia. But on that sunny September morning he failed to see his apparent misfortune in quite the same light. As his parachute opened a strap became entangled with the harness and was pulled tightly under his chin. In this unhappy state he came down to earth, narrowly missing a barrage balloon on the way down, and eventually landing in a cow pasture. The grazing cattle showed little interest in the arrival of a member of the German Air Force but he was soon accosted by the late Mr Leslie Barnes, a one-armed veteran of the First World War. Again, the police were quickly on the scene and another enemy airman was soon on his way to the Flax Bourton Police Station.

Another witness to the events of this day was Miss Dorothy Cooke, a school teacher, who remembers:

When the heavy crash occurred I was sitting on the school floor with all the children, as instructed by the Education Authority. Immediately the door opened and the school caretaker called for us all to 'come and see'. We ran out and saw the tiny figure of a man coming down by parachute by Failand Church. This crew member, believed to be the navigator, landed in a meadow and the schoolmaster in charge of the evacuated class from West Ham (who were using the Lower Failand Hall as a classroom) was waiting for him.

The German was very young and when the master, the late Mr John Smith, pointed to his gun the German took it from his holster and dropped it. Mr Smith then took off the German's flying helmet and gloves and gave him a cigarette.

By this time police, soldiers and firemen had roared into Failand and the young man was soon taken away. We saw him go past the school, sitting in the back of a car between two armed police.

Before handing in the helmet and gloves Mr Smith brought them into the school for all the children to see and I well remember the excellent quality of both.

The airman seen by Miss Cooke was Oberfeldwebel Alfred Narres, the observer of the G1+DN, and by a process of elimination a fifth airman captured at Failand by Dr G.A. Valentine was Oberleutnant Gottfried Weigel, the pilot and *Kommandant*. Looking out of his window Dr Valentine saw a slowly descending parachute and dashing downstairs he ran into the garden, from where he saw the airman alight some 200 yards distant. Passengers in a stationary bus on the road about 100 yards away also had a grandstand view of the incident. The doctor reached the airman only just before two policemen, Sergeant Davis and another officer of the Portishead Police, who had first gone to the crashed German aircraft a mile or so distant. Finding no one in the wreck they set off in their car along the Failand Road to capture the German officer and soon he too was on his way to Flax Bourton. Thus, virtually within minutes of their landing on British soil the entire crew was in custody, a remarkable performance.

When Karl Gerdsmeier arrived at Flax Bourton Police Station he recognised two German parachute harnesses that were lying on the floor and his spirits rose when he heard the familiar voice of Oberleutnant Weigel speaking in unfamiliar English. Entering an inside room a broad smile came over his face when he saw that Karl Geib was there too. An Englishwoman, believed by Geib to have been either a secretary or, perhaps, the wife of one of the policemen, was preparing some food and shortly afterwards Narres also arrived. All four were then given tea, food and cigarettes, and they conversed freely between themselves and with their captors. As a result they were quick to recover from the shock of their recent ordeal.

Meanwhile, at an army transit camp at Shirehampton,

between Bristol and Avonmouth, Sergeant-Major A.H. Richards was ordered by the Camp Commandant to take an armed escort to the Somerset police station to collect the German airmen. While this was going on there were several telephone calls to Flax Bourton, one giving news of Engel's admission to hospital, which was relayed to the other Germans, and another asking whether the Heinkel had been shot down by flak or fighters. Weigel acted as interpreter on these occasions, but the friendly atmosphere ended abruptly with the arrival of the soldiers from Shirehampton.

When the troops saw the Germans, sitting comfortably, sipping tea and smoking, they 'reacted quite strongly' to quote Gerdsmeier. Sergeant-Major Richards and his men were incensed at the cosy scene, for specific instructions had been issued to all concerned about the methods to be adopted when handling German prisoners – they were to be searched, their personal possessions confiscated, and then separated and kept in isolation until interrogated by a local Intelligence Officer of the RAF. Separation, as interpreted by the army, even meant sending four cars, one for each prisoner, and in consequence the soldiers were understandably annoyed at the degree of fraternisation they found.

Sergeant-Major Richards remembers the German pilot as a 'typical Nazi, arrogant and constantly clicking his heels as he gave the Nazi salute* every few minutes.' The convoy of cars took the German airmen to the Tithe Barn at Shirehampton where they were interviewed by Major Gonne, the Camp Commandant, his Garrison Adjutant and Captain Richards of the Camp Staff. Upon arrival Weigel demanded an officer escort, to which he was apparently entitled, but the four men were made to stand in the gravel courtyard, well apart and each guarded by two armed soldiers. Richards thought they suddenly looked apprehensive, and then he realised they probably thought they were about to be shot. A large crowd gathered outside the barn

---

* This salute, the raising of the right arm in the *Deutsche Gruss* or German Greeting, was greatly despised in Britain and was seen as the sure sign of a Nazi. (Note: This was not the Luftwaffe salute, which was the bending of the right arm to touch the right side of the forehead in the usual military manner).

and the British NCO wisely placed a guard on the back entrance to the yard, believing the angry crowd might attack the airmen.†

Continuing his account of events Karl Gerdsmeier remembers:

> We stood in a stony little yard, which I felt particularly as I was wearing a flying boot on one foot and only a sock on the other. An iron staircase led up from the yard to a room and after a while Oberleutnant Weigel was taken up for questioning. After some time a soldier brought me a piece of sacking to wrap around my boot-less foot. My injured knee was now badly swollen and the pain was quite severe.
>
> One after the other we were made to go up the stairs. After Weigel it was Geib's turn, but no sooner had he gone into the room than he re-appeared, bundled out the door and back down the stairs by clearly wrathful soldiers. He was then thrust back up again – My God, I thought, what now?
>
> When my turn came I went up the staircase, feeling very uneasy, and entered the room. Soldiers were at the door and beside a desk. Oberleutnant Weigel was standing at the back of the room by the window and as I entered he made a sign to me, clearly indicating that I should not salute. At this I realised why the previous man had been thrown out – he had saluted by raising his right arm in the *Deutsche Gruss*. This, called the Nazi Salute by the British, was like a red flag to a bull to them!
>
> A man dressed in civilian clothes and speaking an understandable German, asked me some questions, but we had agreed beforehand that we would answer no questions, except to give our names and home addresses.

After about $1\frac{1}{2}$ hours the German airmen were taken to the Central Police Station at Bridewell, Bristol, for overnight detention. Again, they were taken in four cars, each containing a

† There were reports at the time that one of the German airmen had opened fire with a 'Tommy gun' on two farmers as he descended by parachute, but no evidence has come to light to support this. Only Luger P 08 pistols were carried by the crew members concerned and none admitted using them.

prisoner, driver and two armed guards. Gerdsmeier's car was driven by an ATS girl who, wittingly or unwittingly indulging in applied psychology, slowed down in the centre of Bristol to point out a captured Bf 109E fighter that was on display in Broad Quay in connection with the city's War Weapons Week exhibition.

At Bridewell the airmen were accommodated in four cells, but during the night there was a disturbance when a fire was started in one of them by Karl Geib. Incredibly he had managed to retain some papers on his person and he was able to destroy them before the police could extinguish the fire. The prisoners were then moved to other cells but later that night Narres was taken away for interrogation in London – as the observer it was presumed he would know something about a German radio beam navigation system which was of prime interest to RAF Air Intelligence. Early the next morning the remaining prisoners were taken to the railway station under armed escort on the next stage of their journey into captivity. They first went to Swindon POW Transit Camp and from here the NCOs went to Oldham and Weigel to the officer's camp in the Lake District.

Examination of the crashed Heinkel by officers of the RAF's AI 1(g) Branch revealed only a few items of interest, perhaps the most important being the markings G1+DN painted on the fuselage sides. This revealed to a well informed Air Intelligence Branch that the aircraft belonged to 5/KG 55, thereby identifying one of the units involved in the attack. Traces of only three MG 15 machine-guns were found, so the full armament of the aircraft was not established. A manufacturer's plate led the investigating officers to believe that the machine had been built under licence by Land und See Leichtmetall GmbH of Kiel, but actually this referred only to an airframe component. The manufacturer's final assembly plate, riveted externally to the nose of the aircraft and indicating the factory and the aircraft's work's number, was never found by the RAF and only came to light nearly thirty years later when Mr V.C. Harrison of Nailsea, near Bristol, revealed that as a young souvenir hunter he had prised it from a piece of wreckage on the crash site. His memento – surely the envy of any schoolboy in 1940 – shows that the

G1+DN had been built by the Ernst Heinkel Flugzeugwerke GmbH at Rostock. A He 111 P it had the Werke Nummer 2126 and had been accepted by the Luftwaffe on 14th April 1939.

Many were the rumours circulating in the Bristol area about this aircraft; one claimed that it was a Filton-built British bomber captured by the Germans at Dunkirk, another that its pilot was an Old Boy of Bristol's Clifton College. The most widely held belief of all, however, was that the attack was led by a German who had been employed by the Bristol Aeroplane Company before the war. Thus, it was believed, not only did he possess an intimate knowledge of the factory, but he was able to pinpoint precisely the location of the air raid shelters. And to this day there are people living in Bristol who firmly believe this to be true.

The final assembly plate of G1+DN.

IX

Unwelcome Guests – 2

More drama was to be found at Woolverton, about twenty miles
south-east of Failand, where Hauptmann Helmut Brandt's He
111 came down. Here the excitement was centred on Church
Farm, then farmed by Mr Leslie Matthews. The Woolverton
farmer was at market at the time of the crash, but his wife
Gladys was a witness to the event and she recalls that four of the
five men in the crew managed to jump from their burning
bomber, but they were too low and three were killed. A fifth man
failed to get out and his body was burnt beyond recognition in
the wreckage. The only survivor was the pilot, Helmut Brandt,
and he was badly wounded.

Tom Meadway, it will be recalled, checked on the safety of his
family and then went to the crash site near the War Memorial,
beside the Bath-Frome road, where the German bomber was
burning fiercely. As he ran across the field he came across a
German airman lying on the ground. He was alive and
conscious, but badly wounded in several places by machine-gun
bullets. Meadway disarmed the airman, asking him if he spoke
English. The German replied that he understood a little and told
Meadway in halting English how to remove the magazine from
his loaded pistol.

Another man arrived on the scene and between them the two
Englishmen made the wounded airman comfortable, using his
parachute as a pillow. He had two bullets through his right leg,
his right hand was badly shot through and he appeared to have a
neck wound. Tom Meadway lit a cigarette and placed it between
the German's lips, an act that caused some of the women now
present to become quite hostile. The German told Meadway that
his name was Brandt and that he was the pilot of the aircraft and
in response to further questioning revealed that it was his first

time in England and that he had a wife and daughter in Munich.

Brandt then noticed one of his crew lying on the ground about thirty yards away, obviously dead, and asked Meadway to check on his badges of rank. From this the German officer was able to deduce the identity of the dead man.

Recounting what followed Tom Meadway said:

By now a small crowd had gathered and I was kneeling by Brandt who had become worried by some of the remarks being made. These comments, mainly by the women present, were to the effect that he had been killing women and children. To this Brandt replied that he was only doing his duty, as our airmen were doing their duty over Germany. At this point I rebuked the crowd for their behaviour towards an enemy who was no longer a danger to us.

Recalling his impression of Brandt he continued:

There was nothing of the so-called 'arrogant Nazi' about him. He was dignified and although nervous, as one would expect from anyone in his position, he gave an impression of great courage, despite being surrounded by a hostile crowd while in a badly wounded condition and in an obvious state of shock. One other incident remains clearly in my mind – a member of the Home Guard arrived, in civilian clothes but carrying a rifle, and took up a position at Brandt's feet. The German officer turned to me and said, 'Is he going to shoot me?', to which I replied that we didn't do that to prisoners-of-war in England and that he was safer now than when he had been in the air. The final episode of the drama is one that still makes me feel ashamed; an ambulance finally arrived and Brandt was literally bundled in and driven off across the field at a speed which caused the rear wheels to leave the ground and must have caused the wounded man great distress. It was obviously done quite deliberately.

Such was the attitude of the British towards German airmen at that time – compassion by some, hatred by others. Brandt, who

Walter Scherer's Bf 110 C4 (W Nr 3591), the 3U+GS of 8/ZG 26 shot down at Well Bottom near Boyton, Wiltshire, on 25th September 1940. Note the personal insignia carried on the nose.

was thirty-three years old, recovered from his wounds to spend to rest of the war as a POW. The four members of his crew who died were buried in Box Cemetery with full Military Honours, the Vicar of Box, who was also the chaplain of No 10 Group HQ, officiating.

Like Weigel's aircraft, Brandt's G1+EP was a Heinkel 111 P powered by two Daimler-Benz DB.601 engines. Its markings were not decipherable by investigating RAF officers, but their examination of the remains produced a number of maker's plates which revealed that parts of the airframe were produced by Allgemeine Transport GmbH of Leipzig, by the Norddeutsche Dornier Werke and by Ernst Heinkel at Rostock. Only three MG 15s were found but the armour plating appeared to be standard.

Thirteen-years-old John Taylor had just left school for his mid-day lunch break when Walter Scherer's Bf 110 forced-landed near Greatridge Wood, Boyton. Later, with school finished for

Walter Scherer in Düsseldorf, August 1940.

the day, he cycled from his home in Fonthill Bishop to see the German fighter. He remembers that it was in a remarkably good condition and from some men that he knew he heard the story of how the German pilot was captured. The men were timber cutting in Greatridge Wood at the time and they were the first to get to the crash. They could see the pilot moving about in his cockpit and wondered what his intentions might be. While they were debating what to do an army Bren-gun Carrier arrived to solve their problems. The soldiers from the tracked vehicle removed the gunner from the rear cockpit, wrapping him in his parachute for he was clearly dead.

The timber cutters need have had no worries about Walter Scherer for he was in no condition to harm them. In addition to his head wounds he had a fractured skull, a wrenched and badly bruised spine, two crushed ribs and a broken left leg. A broken tooth had badly cut his mouth and congealed blood from his head wounds obscured his vision. He was lifted from his aircraft and taken to hospital in Warminster where, he later recalled, he was extraordinarily well treated. His transfer to a military hospital near Shaftesbury a few days later was, as might be expected, a move for the worse, but he was nevertheless well cared for. After spending three months in hospital Scherer was transferred to a POW Camp at Oldham in Lancashire and later went to Canada. He never fully recovered from his injuries and was recommended for repatriation to Germany in exchange for badly wounded British prisoners of the Germans, but this failed to materialise.

Walter Scherer's Bf 110 C4 was typical of the colourful German fighter aircraft of the Second World War. It was painted in the usual two shades of dark green on its upper surfaces and was light blue underneath. The markings 3U+GS (with the 'G' in red and the remainder in black) revealed its unit to the RAF as 8/ZG 26. It also had red propeller spinners and, as a quick aid to in-flight recognition by other German pilots, an all-white nose section forward of the front cockpit. Yellow stripes on its tail proclaimed to the initiated that it belonged to III Gruppe and the ten bars on its fins signified the number of combat victories claimed by its pilot. On the nose appeared the Red Devil personal insignia of Walter Scherer who was twenty-four years old and a holder of both the Iron Cross First and Second Class (EK I and II).

The body of Gefreiter Heinz Schumacher, Scherer's wireless operator/gunner, was first taken to Warminster but he was later buried with the usual Military Honours at Salisbury.

Military Honours were also accorded to the four German airmen killed at Poole in the crash of the He 111 G1+LR. Its pilot, Oberleutnant Hans Bröcker, the *Staffelkapitän* of 7/KG 55, and another officer in the crew, Oberleutnant Heinz Scholz, were buried at Parkstone Cemetery, together with two NCO crew members. When their aircraft crashed into the large cliff-side house in Branksome Park only a maid was indoors at the time and she escaped unharmed. Perhaps even more fortunate was the gardener who was trimming a hedge as the Heinkel ploughed into the garden. Burning petrol set part of the house on fire and through the roar of flames came the crackle of exploding machine-gun ammunition. Occasionally red pyrotechnic flares also shot into the air from the blazing remains of the aircraft which proved to be a He 111 H with Junkers Jumo 211 engines. In a very short time firemen, military personnel, police, ambulance men, ARP Wardens and members of the public were all at the scene. The house, the remains of the aircraft and some pine trees adjoining the property all burned fiercely with acrid fumes arising from the wreckage.

The fire was soon brought under control but it was some time before firemen recovered the charred remains of twenty-nine-years-old Hans Bröcker, the second *Staffelkapitän* of KG 55 to be lost on this operation. The other four members of his crew, which was unusual in that it included a second officer, had jumped from their crashing aircraft but only Unteroffizier Kurt Schraps, the twenty-one-year-old wireless operator, survived.

Schraps was one of two crew members who alighted by parachute in the sea about 100 yards from the shore and close to a Poole Corporation boat, the crew of which was working on the outfall with a diver. Mr L.W. Trew, an Engineer with Poole Corporation, was in charge of diving operations off Branksome Chine that day and he remembers:

Unteroffizier Kurt Schraps, sole survivor of the He 111
shot down at Poole, 25 September 1940.

The air raid sirens sounded and at once we hoisted the diver
and waited. After a time the sound of aircraft was heard and
then the sky was filled with bombers and fighters and various
dog-fights were going on. The bombers were returning to
France and as we watched someone shouted, 'Look out!' and I
saw a Heinkel 111 coming over the cliffs, on fire and heading
straight for the boat. When only about 500 yards away it
turned and went into the cliff top, exploding into a mass of
flames and demolishing Lady Waverly's house.

I was stood on a seat at the stern and recognising the
aircraft as a Heinkel gave a cheer, shouting 'Hooray, it's
German!'. Turning round I found all the crew with their
heads under the seats!

As the aircraft turned something left it, and then two
parachutes opened, being carried out to sea by the

Schraps falling into the sea in Poole harbour.

momentum. At once I jumped into the small dinghy we were towing and accompanied by Mr E. Wheeler and Mr Sheppard rowed to pick up the airmen.

We came across a German in full flying kit, trying to keep afloat, and took him aboard, taking his Mauser*, helmet, parachute, etc. He was of stocky build, full of face and appeared to be grateful at being saved from a watery grave. We then rowed to the other parachute but the body attached to it was submerged; catching the parachute we brought the man aboard and I noticed that he was shot through the neck and, I believe, in the chest. I then rowed ashore and handed them over to the military.

Another member of the crew was seen by people in Poole to be

* It is more likely that this was a Luger P 08, the standard pistol issued to Luftwaffe aircrew in 1940.

hanging motionless, head slumped forward, as he descended by parachute to land on a railway embankment. He was found to be dead from bullet wounds and it was later established that he was Oberleutnant Heinz Scholz, the observer. The fifth member of the crew, Unteroffizier Günter Weidner, fell to his death when his parachute failed to open; his body was found in Alexandria Road, Parkstone, two miles or so from his crashed aircraft. In another part of the town a pair of German flying boots was found, one of them badly torn and bearing a 1938 date stamp.

Schraps was brought ashore under the gaze of a number of spectators who gathered silently, overlooking the beach at Branksome Chine to watch proceedings. Nearby lay the body of the Heinkel's gunner, Unteroffizier Josef Hanft, covered with a soaking parachute and surrounded by a group of soldiers. The sole survivor was obviously disturbed by the experience he had just been through and he neither spoke nor looked at anyone as he was escorted to a military truck. As he marched along the sands in his white stockinged feet water was still dripping from his saturated blue-grey uniform, in the button-hole of which could be seen the red, white and black ribbon of the Iron Cross, Second Class.

Kurt Schraps was shot down on his 16th operational flight over England. Most of his previous attacks had been carried out at night and while he and his colleagues disliked flights which started after midnight and continued until nearly dawn, it was operations over Britain in daylight that most concerned them. The British fighters, he felt, were most efficient and he respected them very much. Schraps had joined the Luftwaffe in 1938 and upon completion of his training as a wireless operator/gunner took part in the invasion of Poland and France.

Over France he had been shot down and injured, for which he later received the Wound Badge (*Verwundeten Abzeichen*), and was also awarded both the EK I and EK II. Upon recovering from his injuries he rejoined his unit at Villacoublay to participate in the offensive against Britain.

Recalling the moment that his aircraft was first damaged Schraps said:

(Left) Unteroffizier Günter Weidner, flight mechanic of the He 111 shot down at Poole, 25 September 1940. (Right) Unteroffizier Kurt Schraps.

We were hit by a Spitfire before we got to our target and our only wish then was to get back to France as quickly as possible. However, we were not to be granted this wish because we were further badly damaged by a Hurricane just before we reached the Channel coast. The machine caught fire and the *Kommandant* gave the order to bale out. I jumped and landed in the Channel with Hanft. We were rescued by civilians in a boat but my colleague was already dead.

I was handed over to an army unit and taken in a lorry to a villa near the coast. I was well treated there and learned later that my other three comrades were also dead. In the villa my clothes were dried and about two hours later an RAF officer arrived and began questioning me, telling me first of all that I was the only survivor. I was treated very well and I was in no way, physically or mentally, harmed. While there I gave some of my German money to the British soldiers as souvenirs and the remainder was handed back to me when I was discharged after the war.

The following day I was taken by a sergeant to London, via Portsmouth, and went on to an Interrogation Centre by motor-cycle combination. There I was constantly questioned, even at midnight. At first I was in a room by myself and then I was allowed to join some more prisoners in a larger room. We were all moved later to a camp in Oldham.

Later, like so many other POWs, Schraps was moved to a prison camp in Canada, but of his journey to Oldham from London he recalls:

I was not treated with kid-gloves; civilians spat at me and threw stones and, needless to say, I felt very depressed during my first few days as a POW.

Not far from Poole, at Studland near Swanage, lay the wreck of another He 111, the G1+BH of 1/KG 55 flown by Feldwebel Fritz Jürges who, as previously recounted, crash-landed his badly damaged aircraft in a mangold field. This was at Westfield Farm and the first people to arrive on the scene were Mr Theo Janku, the head wine waiter of a Bournemouth hotel, his wife and Mrs Marshallsay of Studland. Mr Janku, a small, bespectacled man of Czech origin, had lived in Britain for many years and spoke no less than five languages. Recalling the incident he reported:

Mrs Janku was halfway across the first field before the plane ceased slithering along and as four Germans scrambled out of the machine she met them. They were holding up their hands when I came up, fifty paces behind my wife as I had stopped to pick up a Home Guard rifle. This, by the way, was not loaded. One of the Germans had hurt his spine and collapsed onto the ground. I told them to hand over their revolvers, which they did readily, but when I told them, again in German, to sit down and take it easy they stood dumbfounded at hearing their own language in rural Britain and I had to order them again to do as they were told.

All relaxed then, except the pilot. Calling out to me that he had left a badly wounded man in the plane, he tried to get back to it. Covering him with my empty rifle I ordered him back – I would have no tricks with the plane and we would lift out his mate if there was one.

About a dozen workmen came running down the hill, brandishing spades and picks which they dropped when they saw that two Germans were hurt. They then did their best to make them comfortable.

Handing the rifle to Mrs Janku, I got two of the workmen to help lift out the rear gunner from the bottom of the plane where he had been thrown from his seat on landing. His thigh was torn and the bone was shattered. After some agonising work we got him out and made him ready for the Medical Officer who, with the ambulance, was not long in coming. The RAF men who took over thought there were live bombs on board and this made us move our patient faster than would otherwise have been the case, but he died half an hour later.

Another early arrival on the crash site was Mr J.P.H. Warner, a member of the Home Guard who, elaborating further, said:

As I approached the plane I found the people from the nearby bungalow and a RAF corporal had already got the men out. One, the rear gunner I think, was badly wounded with his side bleeding profusely from the machine-gun fire from the Spitfires now circling overhead. The officer, whom I took to be the pilot, was older than the rest of the crew who were NCOs and only about nineteen to twenty-one years of age. The officer, stocky and dark, was about thirty-two. I made him take off his jacket so that I could feel his pockets and make sure that he had no weapon on him. He was wearing a thinnish, well-tailored shirt, possibly silk, and his personal identity disc was of a superior type. After a few minutes standing about he said that he was cold and wanted his cap which was still in the plane. He said he would go and fetch it but I at once put myself between him and the plane, holding my rifle towards him and saying that I would fire if he tried to go back. One of the other crew members said, in fairly good

G1 + BH crash-landed at Studland, near Swanage, by Feldwebel Fritz Jürges.

English, 'He is an officer and must have his hat', but I told him to tell the officer that we did not trust him and that all he wanted to do was to set fire to the aircraft.

By this time a small crowd had gathered and we all seemed to be drinking cups of tea and smoking cigarettes, my sister helping the Marshallsays from the bungalow with the distribution. The Germans obviously thought this was great and my sister told them in rather poor German that this was a Christian act and, being a clergyman's daughter, she had been brought up to be merciful to enemies. Soon afterwards the MO arrived to tend to the wounded German, quickly followed by a detachment of the Suffolk Regiment, stationed in Studland, with their commanding officer, Colonel Keating. The British officer shouted to the gathering public to 'Get to hell out of it', emphasising quite angrily that this was 'a war, not a bloody peepshow'. The crew was then taken to a house called Hill Close, the battalion headquarters of the Suffolk Regiment. One of the crew was kept at Hill Close and two days later when we buried the dead gunner in the churchyard, he attended, representing the Luftwaffe – he stood by the grave, obviously distressed, and gave the formal Nazi salute. A firing party was provided by soldiers of the Suffolk Regiment.

The aeroplane remained there for several days before the dismantling crew arrived with a large transporter. I think they were from Morris Motors, Oxford.* Then came the tragedy – as they hoisted up one dismantled wing, it touched the overhead cable and two men were killed instantly. A third was severely burned.

Mrs Marshallsay remembers that one of the crew, a big man with fair, curly hair, was covered in blood and when they cleaned him up as well as they could he appeared to be quite unwounded, the blood apparently having come from his badly injured comrade. During its stay near her bungalow, Mrs Marshallsay charged people to see the aeroplane and collected £60 for the local Spitfire Fund, a scheme to raise cash for the purchase of fighters for the RAF.

The recollections of the German crew members follow closely those of their captors. Karl Köthke recalls that the impact on landing temporarily stunned most of the crew. When he recovered he climbed out of the aircraft to find a woman pointing a rifle at him and telling him to raise his hands.

I could do nothing [he said] but raise them. And then an unbelievable thing happened. The woman, who I am almost certain was the wife of a clergyman, put her rifle down against a tree, took out a packet of cigarettes and offered me one. In the meantime my crew had recovered consciousness, except for the flight mechanic who by now was already possibly dead. They crawled out of the machine, but all had back injuries of some sort due to the heavy landing. They lay on the ground and were later taken to hospital for treatment.

By now I could see Home Guard men coming along with

---

* The aircraft recovery crew belonged to the civilian operated No 50 Maintenance Unit, Cowley, Oxford. From Studland this He 111 was taken to Cardiff where it was re-assembled and placed on exhibition alongside a Spitfire in Cathays Park in connection with the city's War Weapons Week.

Hauptman Karl Köthke (centre front), Kommandant of the He 111 shot down at Studland, 25 September 1940. (Taken while a POW in Canada).

guns waving and in a short time I once again had my hands above my head, with pistols in my back and chest. A little later I was taken by two officers to an Officers' Mess where I was placed under the guard of two armed officers. In the afternoon I was taken downstairs and, to my surprise, I was met by the commanding officer who introduced me to the other officers! We sat around the fireplace and had tea. One officer spoke perfect German and acted as interpreter; he told me that he had a friend living in Germany and that he spent all his holidays in Fischerhude near Bremen. I went to school in Bremen and therefore knew the village well.

Köthke had entered military service in 1926, had been with the Luftwaffe since its early undercover years and held the combined pilot/observer flying badge. His wireless operator, Gefreiter Rudolf Weisbach, was only twenty years old and more than thirty years later has clear recollections of that 25th September. He said:

After landing we tried to get the wounded Altrichter out of the aircraft; we then planned to set fire to our aircraft for in spite of the belly landing it was relatively undamaged. The opportunity did not arise, however, for we were approached by some civilians from a house about five hundred yards away. They were armed and took our pistols away. Some ten minutes later a lady brought some tea for the wounded; the pilot and gunner Flieger Otto Müller were slightly hurt on landing but Altrichter was in a serious condition. After about ten minutes the military came and took us away in vehicles, but for Altrichter it was already too late.

Weisbach was detained in the area for a while and it was he who attended Altrichter's funeral at Studland. Two days later he again represented his Service at the burial of the two members of a Bf 110 crew that died in a crash near Wareham. Weisbach was also the airman whose face, covered in blood, was wiped clean by Mrs Marshallsay, but it was not, he said, the blood of Josef Altrichter. In fact he had cut his finger when replacing a magazine on his MG 15 machine-gun and although it was only a small cut it bled profusely. However, only the pilot, Fritz Jürges, and gunner Otto Müller, the youngest member of the crew, were officially classed as wounded and transferred to hospital.

Fritz Jürges, another experienced, long-serving pilot, was not without a sense of humour. Looking back to his early days in the Luftwaffe he recalls: 'In the early Thirties we were called 'parrots' – we had beautiful feathers (our uniforms), we had big beaks, and we couldn't fly!' He has many amusing tales to tell of those days; he recalls, too, his unauthorised low flying around the statue on a hilltop near Detmold. 'Hermann's Memorial', he calls it, adding, 'not Göring, but the one that fought the Romans under Varus!' Low flying was then a serious offence, forbidden because of the high number of accidents that resulted, but this did not stop Jürges who had a penchant for 'shooting-up' trains. For the attack on Filton his usual observer, a man he did not particularly like, was replaced by Köthke, and Weisbach was standing-in for his regular wireless operator who was on leave. Eighteen-year-old Otto Müller was a recent addition, so only flight mechanic Josef Altrichter remained of his normal crew.

Studland crash survivors. Flieger Otto Müller (sitting, second from left); Gefreiter Rudolf Weisbach (standing, third from left); and Feldwebel Fritz Jürges (standing, fourth from left). (Taken while POWs in Canada).

In addition to the usual unit and identification markings, the G1+BH carried on its fuselage near the wing root a large, white-painted buffalo. Explaining the story behind this, Fritz Jürges recalls:

> In 1939 our *Staffelkapitän* at Langendiebach, Hauptmann von Casimir, founded the Büffel-[Buffalo]Staffel, and all the aircraft of 1 Staffel became adorned with the buffalo insignia. All the rest were painted brown and were bulls, as could be clearly seen! Mine, however, was white and was a cow, the only one in the whole *Staffel*.

The same off-beat sense of humour led the German pilot to refer to his aircraft as 'HMS' G1+BH.

Jürges had wrenched his back quite badly in the crash landing and after a few days in a local field hospital he was transferred to St Herbert's Hospital at Woolwich. From here he went to the London Cage, the POW Transit Camp overlooking Hyde Park, where he was interrogated by the army, and thence to the POW

Camp at Oldham. In 1941 he was shipped to Canada, as were most German prisoners held in Britain.

Examination of the crashed aircraft by the RAF revealed that its starboard Jumo 211A engine had been hit and bursts of 0.303 inch machine-gun fire were evident in the wings and about midway along the fuselage. An oil pipe to the other engine was fractured. Its armament was found to be six MG 15s and its radio and other equipment were standard. The usual bomber camouflage colours were carried but its white spinners and light blue under-surface were covered with 'lamp black', the temporary night flying finish officially termed Flieglack 7120 11 in the German Air Force. It was a recently built He 111 H, according to RAF crash investigators, powered by two Jumo 211A engines, but German records list it as a He 111 P.

Some useful information was obtained from the twelve prisoners and from the wreckage of the five crashed aircraft. It was discovered, for instance, that the assembly of the formation and the subsequent attack had gone exactly as planned. Also revealed were the units taking part, their bases, and the route to and from the target. Documents, including a diary, were found on some of the captured airmen and provided British Air Intelligence with much useful information about the recent activities of KG 55. A target map found in one of the aircraft provided confirmation that the target was GB 73 52, the engine works of the Bristol Aeroplane Company, and a pencilled arrow showed the intended direction of attack and the disposition of the three *Gruppen*. This document also gave an insight into the enemy's knowledge of the Filton plant.

In one of the aircraft a document dated 1st April 1940 was found which stated that explosive ammunition was only to be used against aircraft targets. Its use against troop concentrations and other living targets was expressly prohibited. Similar instructions had only previously been found in the possession of captured German fighter pilots.

Much of the information was obtained from the prisoners by the use of clever interrogation and by means of ruses adopted by the POW Interrogation Unit. In the early years of the war few

German airmen willingly gave away information, but skilful interrogation based on gentle persuasion, supported by eavesdropping by means of hidden microphones, the use of 'stool-pigeons', and other subtleties, produced a great deal of valuable information.

X

Claim and Counterclaim

In the twisting turmoil of air combat it was impossible to determine the outcome of every encounter with any degree of certainty. All too often a victim claimed destroyed managed to return to its base, as a study of losses on the one side and claims on the other reveals. Not only were claims on both sides inflated but incorrect identification of types and, in some cases, honest lack of positive identification, were common. This confusion was experienced by all the participants in the Second World War and increased with the size of the forces involved to reach a climax with the massive American daylight raids over Germany later in the war.

At first twenty German aircraft were claimed destroyed, 18 of them being credited to the fighters, one to the AA guns and another shared by guns and fighters, but in a later report the claims soared to twenty-six. A typical headline proclaimed: 'Nazi Raiders Paid Heavily For Attack On Bristol', but no doubt the inflated figures served to boost a flagging morale and, accordingly, when the search for the wreckage of German aircraft revealed obvious discrepancies in the claims, no attempt was made to correct them.

A study of German records leaves no doubt that RAF claims in this action were exaggerated, as indeed they were throughout most of the Battle of Britain, but the Germans were similarly guilty. One Spitfire was claimed destroyed by the He 111s of KG 55, while five Spitfires and Hurricanes were claimed by the Bf 110s of ZG 26 and two Spitfires by the Bf 109s of I/JG 2. In fact, instead of the eight British fighters claimed shot down, two Spitfires and a Hurricane were lost (Category 3) while lesser damage (Category 2 and 3) was sustained by four aircraft. Only one British pilot was killed.

Those combats that can be positively linked to crashed German aircraft have already been described, but mention must also be made of other claims, most of which probably resulted in damage to the enemy. One such combat was that reported by Pilot Officer Urwin-Mann who, besides contributing to the destruction of the He 111 at Studland, also claimed the destruction of another aircraft of the same type.

He 111s were also claimed destroyed by another two pilots of No 238 Squadron, Pilot Officer Vernon Simmonds and Flying Officer W. Rozycki. With Squadron Leader Harold Fenton and Pilot Officer A.R. Kings each claiming damage to He 111s, the squadron's claim totalled six He 111s destroyed and two damaged.

All the pilots of 238 Squadron correctly reported their adversaries as He 111s, but the pilots of No 609 Squadron claimed some types that can only be explained by faulty aircraft recognition. Flying Officer John Dundas claimed a Do 17 destroyed, Sergeant J. Hughes Rees claimed a Do 215, Flight Lieutenant J.H.G. McArthur a Bf 110, while He 111s were claimed by Flying Officer T. Nowierski and Pilot Officer J. Curchin. The latter also shared with Pilot Officer Wigglesworth of 238 Squadron the claimed destruction of another He 111, presumably the one that crashed at Studland.

Continuing the claims of 609 Squadron, Pilot Officer Keith Ogilvie, a Canadian, claimed a Do 17 destroyed, Pilot Officer M.E. Staples 'probably destroyed' a Bf 110 and Sergeant Alan Feary, who landed at Yeovil following the combat, damaged what he thought was a Do 215. To complete 609's tally, Pilot Officers Miller and Agazarian, as mentioned previously, shared with Urwin-Mann the destruction of the He 111 that crashed at Branksome Park. In cases where Darley's pilots claimed aircraft other than He 111s or Bf 110s, their aircraft recognition was at fault, but such errors were not uncommon; in the heat of battle incorrect identification was common and was by no means restricted to pilots of the Royal Air Force. It should also be borne in mind that from some angles there was a marked similarity between the Bf 110, the Do 17, and the Do 215.

Some of 609 Squadron's claims cannot be substantiated and

clearly some of the enemy aircraft claimed destroyed managed to return to base. Nevertheless, Horace Darley and the thirteen pilots under his command put up a magnificent, aggressive effort, but the squadron commander was scathing in his comments about the tactics adopted by some pilots of other units. He reported seeing some Hurricanes spiritedly attacking one enemy formation, but regretted to say that other friendly fighters were holding back and only attacking stragglers that became separated from the main formation. He quoted three Hurricanes attacking the same disabled enemy aircraft when 'there were plenty of fat targets higher up'.

Of the five British squadrons scrambled to intercept Raid 22, three squadrons and one section of another actually made contact with and engaged the enemy. Two squadrons, Nos 79 and 56, failed to engage and this was entirely due to late orders to take off from Pembrey and Boscombe Down respectively.

Both sides made claims about the results of the attack which were as wide of the mark as the claims of aircraft destroyed. One British newspaper report, after claiming 20 enemy raiders destroyed, stated:

> When the anti-aircraft guns opened fire on the planes they broke formation and tried to reach their objectives singly. The appearance of Spitfires and Hurricanes further disturbed them and dog-fights developed over the town. The crash of bombs shook houses over a wide area and the intense anti-aircraft fire added to the din. Most of the bombs fell in residential areas of the city and although there were a number of casualties, some fatal, many miraculous escapes occurred. Several families were buried under debris and when extracted by demolition squads were found to be uninjured.

Reports of this nature neither soothed the fears of the civil population nor, as was intended, misled the enemy. The public was both concerned and mystified at the apparent ease with which the enemy had completed his task and grave doubts were raised.

The German version of the attack differed considerably and, it must be admitted, was essentially more factual. Their official OKW communiqué and DNB broadcasts claimed:

Formations of the German Air Force bombed the aero-engine works at Filton near Bristol this morning. The attack was made in several waves and the bombers, which were escorted by fighters, scored direct hits on the works. Several air combats ensued but the exact number of enemy aircraft shot down has not yet been ascertained. The last squadrons of our aircraft were able to assess the devastation caused by our bombs. As they left there were thick clouds of smoke over the factory.

German newspapers and magazines carried photographs showing the raid in progress with captions stating 'This factory will not produce many more aircraft.'

The OKW communiqué was based on an intelligence summary prepared by Luftflotte 3 HQ. According to this the flak over Bristol was both intense and accurate, but something of a mystery surrounds the report of a radial-engined fighter of unknown type that was seen over the city. Reputably manoeuvrable, this single-seat fighter was apparently slower than the Bf 110. Equally mysterious were the reports by some German crews that upon exploding some flak shells left broad smoke-like trails suspended in the air at 16,000 feet which left slight marks on the wings of aircraft that flew through them. Both mysteries appear to have no substance for British records throw no light on either phenomenon; almost certainly the first was a result of mis-identification of a Hurricane and the second was probably the effect of the upper wind on the normal smoke left by the explosions of AA shells.

The resistance to the enemy in the Bristol area was clearly not apparent to many spectators on the ground and the seemingly unopposed passage of the raiders led some local residents to conclude that Bristol's defences had been drastically reduced. Protests followed and the local garrison commander, anxious to prevent the spread of unfounded rumour, let it be known that this was not the case, but this did little to reassure the populace.

Bristol's protesting citizens were not alone in their demand to know what had gone wrong, for Lord Beaverbrook, Britain's recently appointed Minister for Aircraft Production, was also concerned at the events of the day. Beaverbrook, after learning that there had been a clear indication of the approaching enemy aircraft forty-seven minutes before the bombing, wanted to know why Fighter Command had failed to prevent the raid. There had been similar attacks against other aircraft factories and the Minister was determined to probe these failures in order to prevent their recurrence.

Presumably Lord Beaverbrook was satisfied with the explanation he received and the proposals to prevent a repetition, but unlike the Minister the people of Bristol, not sharing his knowledge, remained dissatisfied. They knew only that the communiqué issued by the Ministry of Home Security and the reports that appeared in local and national newspapers failed to give a true picture of the raid. However, although serious errors were made by the defenders, the comments and criticisms of the public were not altogether justified.

The alleged absence of opposition was based on what was seen – or what people thought they had seen – of events over Bristol, but the complainants failed to realise that their observations were limited and did not necessarily reflect the true situation. There were, for example, several reports of Bf 109s over Bristol that morning, but because of the short range of these aircraft they must have been Spitfires or Hurricanes. No other single-engined types were involved.

It is certain, however, that on this occasion Fighter Command was not at its best. In response to Lord Beaverbrook's criticism it was admitted by Sir Hugh Dowding, in a letter to the Minister, that 'the 10 Group Controller did not make full allowance for the space and time factors, since the orders he gave to some of his squadrons were too late to bring them into action at the positions indicated.' The Commander-in-Chief of Fighter Command continued: 'He was also starting at a disadvantage, since he had only one squadron at Readiness between Middle Wallop, Exeter, Yeovil and Pembrey.' In extenuation of the 10 Group

Controller it was also pointed out that his Group had only recently been organised, that it did not have the experience of No 11 Group in intercepting mass raids, and that the Group's 'communications and facilities at the time were on a "lash-up" basis'.

It is clearly impossible to say whether or not the bombers would have succeeded in reaching Bristol if all the squadrons had been scrambled in time and more effectively controlled, but it seems more than likely that the majority would have reached the target area. Possibly a lesser weight of bombs might have been delivered – and more enemy aircraft might have been shot down – but earlier interceptions in greater strength might well have resulted in more bombs falling short of the target because of harassment by fighters. And any bombs so jettisoned might well have landed on the built-up residential areas to the south and south-west of the factories, possibly resulting in greater damage and even more casualties; but this is mere conjecture and as such has no real place in this account. Certain, however, is the fact – unpalatable at the time – that the enemy had succeeded in reaching and seriously damaging a key factory in the British aircraft industry.

XI

A Timely Move

There can be little doubt that Air Chief Marshal Sir Hugh Dowding shared Lord Beaverbrook's concern at the events of 25th September for the very next day he issued instructions for the transfer of No 504 (County of Nottingham) Squadron from Hendon to Filton for the express purpose of guarding the Bristol factories from a possible follow-up attack. This was the first time that a squadron had been allocated such a task although, of course, the move also served to bolster the overall defence of the West Country with its other important aircraft factories at Yate (near Bristol), Yeovil and Gloucester.

The pilots of No 504 Squadron, another of the pre-war Auxiliary Air Force units embodied into the RAF in 1939, had experienced mixed fortunes in the past six months. In May 1940 the squadron was sent to France to help stem the German onslaught, but within ten days it was back in the United Kingdom, having lost all but four of its aircraft. During the early stages of the Battle of Britain the squadron was rebuilding its operational strength in Scotland, at the same time helping to protect Scapa Flow, and it was not until 6th September that a move southwards brought its pilots into the thick of the fighting again. Since that date No 504 had seen a great deal of action and had built up a good score of enemy aircraft destroyed. In one day alone (15th September) the squadron was credited with five enemy aircraft destroyed and six damaged. Its move to the West Country to protect an aircraft factory, although unprecedented, was to prove timely.

Seventeen Hurricanes of the squadron left Hendon for Filton at 10.30 hours on 26th September, led by Squadron Leader John Sample. En route they landed at Yatesbury to await the lowering of Bristol's balloons and as a result did not arrive at their new base until 15.00 hours. Before they landed most of the craters on the landing area had been filled in and a number of unexploded bombs removed. An advance party of ground personnel also arrived, flown in by transport aircraft and bringing with them the squadron's bulldog mascot. Their first task upon landing was to refuel and service the squadron's Hurricanes for immediate Readiness.

Meanwhile the rest of the squadron's personnel spent most of the day packing equipment and spares for transport to Filton by road and at 18.00 hours, when all was ready, a convoy of 21 vehicles left the North London airfield to travel through the night to Bristol. After a trying journey through the blackout they arrived at 02.30 hours and the ground crews spent the rest of the night in the coaches and other vehicles in which they had travelled. Most were glad to go for an early breakfast to stretch their limbs, and then started the job of unpacking and settling into new quarters.

On 26th September the Luftwaffe had continued its assault on the British aircraft industry. As already stated, an attack by two *Gruppen* of KG 55 on the Woolston factory seriously affected Spitfire production and served to confirm the enemy's intention to concentrate on aircraft manufacturing centres.

The next day, Friday 27th, dawned bright and clear to open yet another day in the air war over Britain. In Bristol, still shocked from the effects of the Wednesday attack, the sirens had continued to sound repeatedly and at 09.31 that morning there was yet another Alert. It was short-lived, however, being terminated after only thirteen minutes when a Ju 88 of 3 (F)/123, by-passing Bristol on a photographic reconnaissance mission to Liverpool, was intercepted and shot down to make a forced landing on the beach at Porlock Weir on the Somerset coast of the Bristol Channel.

Then, at 11.23, Bristol's sirens were heard once more. Coincidentally with the sirens, orders were received at Filton for 504 Squadron to scramble. Heavy-eyed ground crew, weary from a fitful night spent in the vehicles that had brought them from Hendon, stopped unloading equipment to watch twelve of the squadron's Hurricanes roll across the grass to the eastern boundary of the airfield, turn into wind and start their take-off

Wishful Thinking. A Messerschmitt AG advertisement, depicting the hoped-for success of the Bf 110 fighterbomber.

run in two groups. The first six aircraft became airborne at 11.25, followed closely by the second group. Climbing initially to the west the two Flights quickly joined up and making a left turn climbed on a southerly heading, over the city and into sun.

The scramble was also witnessed by some apprehensive employees of the Bristol Aeroplane Company to whom the warning, so similar in timing to that of Wednesday morning, gave some concern. Almost immediately the Raid Imminent factory warning was given over the Tannoy system and there followed a hurried exodus. The majority rushed to the shelters, but bearing in mind the events of two days ago, some left the works altogether, jumping onto the tailboards of lorries or leaving by foot, car, motor-cycle and bicycle in a bid to escape what many thought was imminent danger. As they fled the distant throb of aircraft engines was again heard and then, approaching from a more southerly aspect this time, a mass of aircraft came into sight. The large formation confirmed to many people living in the south of Bristol that a repeat of the Wednesday raid was about to take place, but events then took a very different turn as British fighters went into action over the city, in full view of its residents, and completely broke up the attack.

For those who did not see the rout the local evening newspapers carried graphic accounts of the action. Typical headlines read: 'Nazi Raiders Put To Flight' and 'Hurricanes Drive Off Mass Raid on S.W. Town – Nine Nazis Shot Down in Rout.' The accounts continued:

Nine of the formation of about 50 planes which attempted to raid a south-west town today were, it is reported, shot down. As they came over a formation of Hurricanes met them and a terrific dog-fight ensued. Several Nazis were shot down after the engagement started and the other planes did a quick about turn and fled for home.

Another report stated:

The raiders could be easily recognised over the south-west town by the light blue of their wings as they turned in the

At Readiness. Flight Lieutenant W. Barrington Royce and two squadron colleagues at Filton, 1940. (504 Squadron).

Pilot Officer Murray Frisby, his Hurricane and groundcrew. Filton 1940.

sunshine. Anti-aircraft guns were quickly in action and British fighters, which had patrolled the town for some minutes before the arrival of the Nazis, wheeled round and attacked. People cheered as the fighters darted around the raiders like wasps round a honey pot.

Further reports in local papers the next day dropped the references to a 'South-West town', a normal security measure, and referred instead to Bristol by name. 'The clash of the two air squadrons over the outskirts of Bristol', stated one newspaper, 'was a tonic for the thousands of people who saw it, and last night and this morning it was the only topic of conversation among workers travelling in the buses.'

There was no doubt among the people of Bristol that the Filton-based Hurricanes had saved the BAC factories and perhaps the city itself from a follow-up attack. Full of admiration for the magnificent performance put up over the city, the employees of the Filton works organised a collection to purchase beer and cigarettes for the squadron as a token of their appreciation. Contributions were readily forthcoming and before long a sizeable sum was to hand. Cigarettes and beer were handed over to the squadron on 28th September and the next day the Lord Mayor of Bristol paid a visit to Filton to personally thank 504's pilots for their gallant efforts. A few days later the employees of the BAC presented the squadron with £39 and another 2,000 cigarettes, much to the embarrassment of the pilots who decided to give some of the cash to the RAF Benevolent Fund. In the spirit of the presentation, however, some of the money was used to buy beer for the squadron's ground crews while the pilots settled for dinner in Bristol.

Recalling this period one of the squadron's pilots, W. Barrington Royce, said:

The carpenters at the Bristol works made-up a cigarette or cigar box, which they filled for us. They also included some money, following a 'whip-round'. It was a marvellous gift – the box was beautifully carved and with cigarettes in short supply it was a gesture we greatly appreciated. Goodness knows where they managed to get them. Some of the money went to the airmen and with some of the remainder we decided to give ourselves a dinner. We went off to the best hotel in Bristol and Murray Frisby, a great food artist, and Mike Rook, our wine connoisseur, concocted a menu that assured us of a really slap-up dinner.

The gratitude of Bristol's citizens made a deep impression on the pilots and ground crews of the County of Nottingham Squadron. It was a gratitude expressed in a variety of ways, as Barrington Royce remembers. Shortly after their arrival at Filton the squadron's pilots started to frequent the Carpenter's Arms public house, then run by a Mrs Jefferies. They used to walk there each evening, a distance of a mile or so each way, and when Mrs Jefferies heard about this she visited neighbours, whose husbands were away in the services, and gathered a collection of bicycles no longer in use. Eight or so were then handed over to the pilots to facilitate their visits to 'the local' and to ease their general transport problems around the airfield. In the words of Barrington Royce, 'they were a godsend to us'.

Writing of the events of that memorable day a local historian* placed on record:

On the 27th, the enemy attempted to repeat his exploit of two days before, but he soon learned his mistake. This time Bristol was ready for him. British fighters scattered the enemy like a flock of sheep and, with the aid of anti-aircraft fire, the assailants were driven off before they could inflict any damage on the city.

The author concluded:

This victory did much to restore public confidence, and that confidence was still further strengthened that same day when the Town Clerk announced that a squadron of fighters was henceforward to be based on Filton.

* C.M. MacInnes, *Bristol at War*, Museum Press, 1962

Station Transport. Squadron Leader John Sample, officer commanding 504 Squadron, with bicycle. Filton, 1940.

Four persons were killed and another injured by bombs that fell at Patchway and Charlton, but not a single bomb fell on nearby Filton – and little wonder for, despite all the assumptions made about this attack, neither Filton nor Bristol were the intended targets. The target was, in fact, the Parnall Aircraft Company factory at Yate, but intercepted near Filton the raiders were obliged to jettison their bombs. Thus, contrary to the popular belief that the British fighters had saved Filton their engagement of the German aircraft over the northern outskirts of Bristol nearly caused bombs to fall there by accident.

But to return to the beginning. The unit given the task of attacking Yate was Erprobungsgruppe 210, the specialist ground attack fighter-bomber *Gruppe* that two days earlier had attacked Portland as a forerunner to the raid on Filton. The Gruppe consisted of two *Staffeln* equipped with Bf 110s and a third equipped with Bf 109s. All were fitted with external bomb racks, but the short range of the 109-equipped Staffel greatly restricted its use and for the attack on Yate only 1 and 2 Staffeln were used.

Even without bombs the Bf 110 was no match for the Spitfires and Hurricanes of Fighter Command and with two 500 kg bombs slung beneath its fuselage the German fighter-bomber's performance was further seriously degraded. It follows that if engaged by British fighters the German pilots were obliged to jettison their bombs if they were to have any chance of survival.

Erprobungsgruppe 210 has been acclaimed by some air war historians as a highly successful 'crack' unit, but a detailed study of their operations during the Battle of Britain does not altogether support this view. The bravery of its crews is not in doubt, but its operations, with a few notable exceptions, produced little more than an incredible saga of near misses, navigational errors, and disastrously high losses. Formed under the command of Swiss-born Hauptmann Walter Rubensdörffer, the unit was originally charged with bringing the new Messerschmitt Me 210 into service, but problems with this aircraft resulted in late deliveries and, originally as an interim measure, fighter-bomber tactics were developed using existing Bf 110 equipment. In July 1940 Erpr Gr 210 became operational as a Luftflotte 2 ground attack unit. It was based at Denain/Valenciennes for much of the offensive over south-east England and the English Channel and then moved to Le Havre and Cherbourg for operations over the south and south-west of England. Its claims during earlier stages of the Battle of Britain are not supported by a study of British bomb damage reports and, in addition, it suffered heavy losses; Rubensdörffer himself was killed on 15th August during an attack in which Croydon was bombed in error for Kenley. Seven aircraft of Erpr Gr 210 were lost that day in what can only be described as a massacre. And the massacre did not stop there – before the Battle of Britain came to an end the unit was to lose three more *Gruppe* commanders and six *Staffelkapitäne*.

On 7th September the strength of the *Gruppe* was twenty-six aircraft of both types; seventeen were then serviceable, but only ten Bf 110s were available for the attack on Yate. They were led

Hauptmann Martin Lutz, Gruppenkommandeur of Erpr Gr
210 and leader of the attack on Yate, 27 September
1940.

by Hauptmann Martin Lutz, the *Gruppenkommandeur* and
successor to Hauptmann von Boltenstern who was killed on 4th
September after succeeding Rubensdörffer.

The ten fighter-bombers were provided with an escort drawn
from all three *Gruppen* of Oberstleutnant Joachim Huth's ZG 26,
the Bf 110-equipped *Zerstörergeschwader* that had provided the
escort for KG 55's attack on Filton on the 25th. Further
supporting and escort missions were flown by Bf 109s of JG 2
and JG 53.

In fighter-bomber attacks of this nature the bomb aiming was
done by the pilot, usually from a low level following a shallow-
dive attack from medium altitude. During the latter stages of the
dive the Bf 110s heavy front armament of cannon and machine-
guns could be used with telling effect. On this particular
operation each aircraft carried two SC 500s and a high level
approach to the target was planned. Such attacks could be quite
devastating against poorly defended targets, but accurate
navigation was not Erpr Gr 210's strong point and the unit
seems to have had problems in pin-pointing inland targets.

Coastal targets were more easily found but accurate pilot-navigation based on map reading while handling a fast aircraft and keeping a watchful eye for opposing fighters was a demanding task, particularly at low altitudes. The wireless operator/gunner could assist to some extent by obtaining radio bearings en route to the target, and for homing purposes on the return flight, but for the approach to the target there was little he could do to assist the pilot from his seat in the rear of the aircraft.

Formerly equipped with Messerschmitt Bf 110 C4s, Erprobungsgruppe 210 had recently received some of the new Bf 110 D variants including some of the very latest D3s. Long-range external fuel tanks were part of their standard equipment but were not always fitted. All, however, were equipped with ETC 500 bomb carriers under the fuselage centre-section for the carriage of 250 or 500 kg bombs. Symbolising their ground attack role the *Gruppe*'s aircraft carried a unit crest that consisted of a yellow ring-type gunsight superimposed over a red map of the British Isles.

Locating their target at Yate should have presented the pilots of Erpr Gr 210 with few problems. Railway lines running west and north from Bristol led directly to Yate airfield, the home of Parnall Aircraft Limited. Although not one of the better known firms in the aircraft industry the company nevertheless played an important part in the war effort. The company was originally formed by George Parnall, a founder member of the Society of British Aircraft Constructors, and was then engaged in aircraft manufacture at the Coliseum Works in Bristol. It moved to Yate aerodrome, situated about ten miles north-east of Bristol, in 1925 and occupied premises originally built in 1916/17 to accommodate the No 3 Aircraft Repair Depot. After the First World War the aerodrome was vacated by the RAF and remained unoccupied until Parnall moved in. Ten years later George Parnall disposed of his business and a new company, formed by the amalgamation of George Parnall and Co., the Hendy Aircraft Co., and Nash and Thompson, Ltd., came into being under the name Parnall Aircraft Limited.

Among those joining the board of the new concern was A.G. Frazer Nash, the well-known racing motorist, who, in association with Captain E. Gratton-Thompson, the new Managing Director, had been involved in the development and manufacture of power-operated gun turrets, a unique feature on many British aircraft, and production of these now became centred on Yate. Perhaps the best known aircraft produced at Yate before the war was the Heck, a light sporting two-seat monoplane that participated in various King's Cup Air Races between the years 1936 and 1950. Other types produced by Parnall Aircraft included the Pixie, Imp and Elf, but sub-contract work played an increasingly important part in the company's output and with the outbreak of the Second World

Parnall Aircraft, Yate. A pre-war photograph.

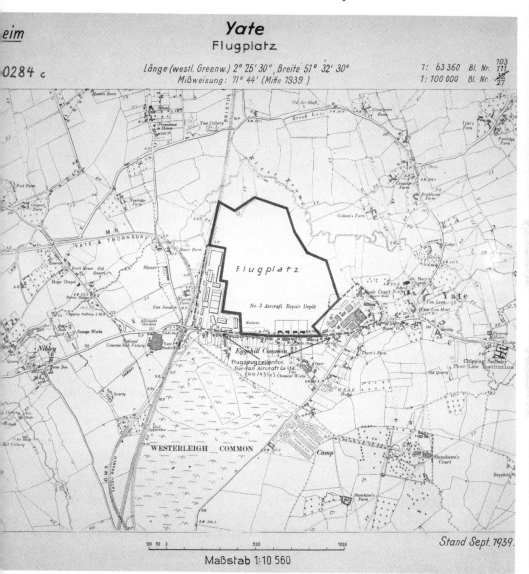

German target documents, Yate airfield (GB 10 284, Yate Flugplatz).

War the factory was further expanded to cope with the manufacture of components for Whitley and Spitfire aircraft. Eventually Parnall Aircraft was to become the largest Spitfire airframe sub-contractor in the country, but in the autumn of 1940 it was with gun turret manufacture that the company was primarily engaged. This was known to German Intelligence for the Luftwaffe's 5 Abteilung included in its target documentation the following:

> This works is the main production centre for twin- and four-gun turrets as used in the tail position of British bomber aircraft. Parnall Aircraft is part of the Nash and Thompson firm and the destruction of this factory would have a serious effect on bomber aircraft production.

It was not difficult for the Germans to acquire information of this type. Guides to British industry often contained such details, as illustrated in the following paragraph which appeared in the British Aircraft Industry number of an aeronautical magazine published in Britain in December 1939, three months after the war started:

> Parnall Aircraft Ltd. – Design and manufacture of aircraft and aircraft components. Specialists in armament equipment for all types of aircraft and manufacturers of the F.N. type of gun turret, developed by Captain A. Frazer-Nash, and adopted by the Air Ministry.

The same magazine gave the company's address, but this was readily available anyway from pre-war advertisements that appeared in the technical press. It is surprising, however, that information on the company's activities should continue to be published by the aeronautical press in time of war.

The Luftwaffe target documents on Yate covered the airfield itself and what German Intelligence thought was still an aircraft repair depot (GB 10 284 Yate Flugplatz mit Aircraft Repair Depot), and the Parnall factories (GB 74 51 Flugzeugzellenfabrik Parnall Aircraft Co. Ltd.). The target maps were based on old British Ordnance Survey maps which labelled part of the buildings 'Aircraft Repair Depot', referring to its First World War rôle, and no doubt it was this that led the Germans to assume its continued use in this capacity.

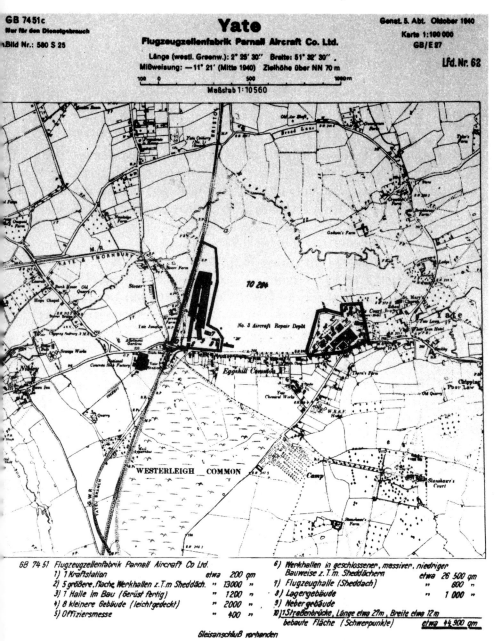

German target documents, Parnall Aircraft Co Ltd, Yate. (GB 74 51 Flugzeugzellenfabrik Parnall Aircraft Co Ltd).

XII

Rout in the Sun

The ten Bf 110s of Erpr Gr 210 took off from Cherbourg at 10.40 hours, in two groups of five with Hauptmann Lutz leading 1 Staffel and Oberleutnant Wilhelm Rössiger leading 2 Staffel. Forming up they set course on a direct track to Yate. Five minutes later forty-two Bf 110s of ZG 26 set off on the same track and unencumbered with bombs soon caught up with the slower fighter-bombers they were to protect. Ahead of the combined force of fifty-two Bf 110s ranged eleven Bf 109s of II/JG 2, hoping to draw off any British fighters attempting to intercept the fighter-bombers over the coast. To cover the return of the attackers and their long-range escort, I and III Gruppen of JG 2 were to take off at 11.25 to meet the returning Bf 110s in the St Albans Head area, twenty-nine Bf 109s of these *Jagdgruppen* joining forces with another seven aircraft of the same type belonging to JG 53. In total, therefore, 89 fighters were to provide protection for 10 fighter bombers, a ratio seemingly more than adequate to ensure a successful penetration of the defences.

Shortly after leaving the Cherbourg Peninsula the German aircraft were observed by the British RDF Stations and the raiders were tracked across the English Channel towards Bournemouth. The symbols on the Fighter Command Operations Room plotting tables showed a force of 'Fifty Plus', but despite the early radar warning there was, for the second time in two days, a delay in dispatching intercepting fighters which again almost resulted in the enemy aircraft reaching their target without serious opposition.

The first aircraft to be scrambled were two Hurricanes of 238 Squadron, ordered to take off from Middle Wallop at 11.00 hours with instructions to patrol overhead their base at 25,000 feet. Shortly afterwards twelve Hurricanes of No 56 Squadron became airborne from Boscombe Down. Led by Squadron Leader Harold Pinfold they too were ordered to climb overhead their base and await further instructions.

At 11.12 hours Red Warnings were issued to coastal areas and at the same time the Hurricanes of 56 Squadron were vectored towards Bournemouth. However, the German formation altered course slightly to cross the coast to the east of Portland where they were ineffectively engaged by the guns defending the naval base. As the fast flying raiders continued inland 56 Squadron was re-directed to Shaftesbury in pursuit, but they were too far away to overtake the German aircraft.

As the enemy formation passed abeam Warmwell at 11.15 twelve Spitfires of No 609 Squadron took off and as they did so elements of ZG 26 were detached from the main escort to circle high above the Dorset airfield, joined by some Bf 109s of II/JG 2. Ten Spitfires of 152 Squadron became airborne from the same airfield four minutes later but one aircraft developed engine trouble and was forced to return and land.

The late instructions to scramble effectively prevented the two Warmwell-based* Spitfire squadrons intercepting the enemy force until it was well inland and, as the squadron's Operations Record Book states, the pilots of 609 Squadron had cause to complain of bad positioning by the Sector Controller for the second time in two days. On this occasion they were first ordered eastwards to patrol Bournemouth at 20,000 feet before they were re-directed to the north-west in pursuit. By an unfortunate coincidence both flight commanders had R/T problems so the lead of the squadron fell to Yellow Section Leader, Pilot Officer R.G. 'Mick' Miller, an Australian with a short service commission in the RAF.

As the German formation approached Frome some more escorting Bf 110s turned away towards the south to take up a 'holding' orbit in the Portland area. In consequence the size of the formation was reduced to something like thirty-five aircraft

* No 609 Squadron was actually based at Middle Wallop but used Warmwell as a forward operating base.

Hurricanes of 56 Squadron.

as it passed over Radstock, from which point the Bf 110 fighter-bombers and their close escort started a shallow dive together towards the target.

The 12 Hurricanes of No 504 Squadron, scrambled at 11.30 with orders to patrol 'Milk B Line' (Filton aerodrome), were led in the absence of their CO by Flight Lieutenant W.B. Royce. Instructed to climb to 20,000 feet they were in a typical but out-moded Fighter Command formation of three 'Vics' of three aircraft (one with an additional Hurricane 'in the box') with two 'weavers' zig-zagging behind the squadron to maintain a look-out for any attack from the rear.

Barrington Royce recalls that his commanding officer, Squadron Leader John Sample, was visiting the Filton Operations Room that morning, leaving himself in charge of the squadron. He further recalls:

Flight Lieutenant W. Barrington Royce, the 504 Squadron formation leader during the attack on Yate, 27th September 1940, with (right) the Squadron Intelligence Officer.

We were in the crew room when Johnny rang to say that a raid was coming in and I queried, 'Why don't we go?' He replied, 'Group say we've got to wait'. Then he came through again to say that they were crossing the coast, to which I replied, 'Well, for God's sake let's get off! What height are they?' He said, '20,000 feet', to which I responded, 'We'll never get up there in time unless we go now!' Anyway, about three or four minutes later the scramble came through. I had already told everybody to start up, so we were actually more or less sitting in the aircraft and waiting to go.

Royce, a Special Reserve and Auxiliary pilot since 1932, had flown Horsley, Wallace and Hind bombers with 504 Squadron before it became a fighter unit in October 1938. He then flew Gauntlets before converting to Hurricanes in 1939 and from the

Waiting to Scramble. 504 Squadron pilots at Readiness, Filton, 1940. They include Sgt Jones (2nd from left), Tony Rook (5th from left), Barry Royce (6th from left) and Murray Frisby (extreme right with back to camera).

outbreak of war had been engaged on flying operations both from bases in the United Kingdom and France. Casting his mind back to 27th September 1940, he remembers:

> We had an awful lot of trouble with the barrage balloons that surrounded Filton. Of course, they were very reluctant to pull them down and when we took off that day they were still only about half lowered; I well remember we had to thread our way through the darned things after we took off, but they were down by the time we got back ... We got off in about a minute, but even then, as it turned out, we were still a couple of thousand feet below the enemy aircraft when we made contact. Fortunately they were then diving or their height advantage would have been greater.

Pilot Officer Murray Frisby of 504 Squadron in the cockpit of his Hurricane Mk I (V6825 TM:F) at Filton.

At 11.45, with the squadron now at 10,000 feet and still climbing, Pilot Officer Murray Frisby, one of the weavers, saw the German aircraft approaching from the rear and warning his formation leader by R/T carried out a climbing turn towards the enemy.

Led by Hauptmann Martin Lutz, the German fighter-bombers had already started their shallow dive from about 25,000 feet and were down to 15,000 and going very fast as they approached Bristol, closely followed by about twenty-five Bf 110s of their escort. Pilot Officer Frisby, still climbing with his throttle wide open, came at the enemy head-on, opening fire on the leading German aircraft which was seen to bank sharply to the left and dive away 'with white streamers from each engine'. Frisby's remarkably gallant action started an incredible break-

Messerschmitt Bf 110 C4 (U8+FK). This unique photograph almost certainly shows the U8+FK flown by Oberfeldwebel Hans Tiepelt with Unteroffizier Herbert Brosig, taken a few days before they were shot down and killed at Fishponds, Bristol, 27 September 1940.

up of the German formation; he almost certainly hit Lutz's aircraft and caused others to turn away in evasive action.

Barrington Royce recalls:

> Murray did a head-on attack – I had shouted 'Individual attacks' over the R/T as it was absolutely hopeless trying to make a combined attack. We went in, but I only seemed to get the chance of an oblique shot at one enemy aircraft, but I obviously hit him because there was no return fire from the gunner.

With characteristic modesty he continued; 'By the time I was finished with that and had a crack at another, I was out of ammunition – and that's all I did that day really.' He landed straight away to re-arm, hoping to take off again immediately to rejoin the fray, but the action was more or less over before he could do so. He reflects:

The trouble, you know, is that everything at the time seems so disjointed – you don't really know what you've done. We didn't know whether they had dropped their bombs, or what had happened. It was all over very quickly.

The entire squadron was close behind Murray Frisby. When first seen the German aircraft were down to about 11,000 feet, just 1,000 feet above the Hurricanes which they were fast overtaking on a similar course. As soon as the British fighters turned into the attack, their opponents swung away to the south-east and started climbing back up to 20,000 feet, hoping that their superior speed, accrued in the shallow dive, would give them a better rate of climb and therefore a height advantage over their adversaries.

Hundreds of people saw the clash of the two groups and the remarkable events that followed. As reported in the press, enemy aircraft scattered in all directions and the enthralled crowds in the streets below cheered and clapped, displaying little regard for their own safety as bullets, spent cartridge cases and shell splinters rained down.

Small groups of the enemy not engaged by fighters were subjected to anti-aircraft fire, the guns adding to the whine and howl of Rolls-Royce and Daimler Benz engines and the staccato rattle of cannon and machine-guns. All semblance of an orderly attack was gone and the pilots of Erprobungsgruppe 210 were forced to jettison their bombs, as they later admitted, and make good their escape.

The hurriedly released bombs fell mainly in open countryside around the outskirts of North Bristol and in the Filton area, causing little damage but inflicting a few casualties, some fatal. Three bombs fell beside the old by-pass at Charlton, wrecking a car and killing its driver. Another man and two children, travelling along the same road in a horse-drawn trap, were also killed.

The pilots of 504 Squadron excelled themselves. Pilot Officer B.E.G. White, like Frisby, also attacked the leading enemy section; turning into the approaching Bf 110s he climbed hard, fired a three seconds burst, stalled and fell away. White,

Oxygen bottles and fuselage wreckage of the Bf 110 shot down at Fishponds, Bristol, 27 September 1940.

nicknamed 'Crasher' following an incident involving a Hurricane at Digby early in the war, recovered from his loss of height and set off in pursuit of the retreating enemy aircraft. Climbing to 20,000 feet he then carried out a second attack, diving from out of the sun onto a Bf 110 flying on the enemy's right flank. The German fighter was seen to dive and then rear up almost vertically before it stalled and continued its dive into the ground in flames.

Flying Officer Michael Royce, the younger brother of 504 Squadron's leader on this occasion, was also in action over Bristol. He reported:

When we attacked the enemy aircraft were approaching Filton at 12,000 feet. They broke formation and started climbing, but I got on to one and fired a burst of three seconds. White smoke came from its port engine. I then noticed an enemy aircraft on my tail and did a steep turn to get onto its tail. I then fired a long burst of nearly ten seconds, and white smoke came from both its engines. The enemy aircraft then dived into the yard of a house in East Bristol, exploded and burst into flames.

This incident was witnessed by many people in the city's Fishponds district, the doomed Bf 110 leaving a long trail of smoke as it dived across the city with the note of its engines rising to a high pitched howl. Close behind was Michael Royce's Hurricane and as the two machines came lower the Messerschmitt burst into flames. From a height of about 6,000 feet its dive steepened and just above roof-top level it broke up. An explosion followed and the entire aircraft disintegrated in a sheet of flame and black smoke. A large piece of burning wreckage struck the roof of 'D' Block of the Stapleton Institution (now Manor Park Hospital) and ricocheted into the courtyard, causing a shallow crater. Most of the wreckage came down in the same yard, amid cascades of burning petrol.

The Fire Brigade was quickly on the scene, aided by the Auxiliary Fire Service, and police and ARP personnel rapidly cordoned off the area. Ammunition exploded in the burning

Bf 110 crash at Fishponds, Bristol.

wreckage, creating a real hazard for the firemen, but the main fear, groundless as it happened, was the possibility of bombs in the wreckage.

Shortly before the crash nurses had been sleeping in 'D' Block, but fortunately they had been roused and evacuated to the air raid shelters when the sirens were heard. No casualties resulted, either among the staff or the inmates of the Institution and damage to the building was slight. In spite of the intense heat and the risk of explosions the fire was quickly extinguished.

The crashed aircraft was the U8+FK of 2/ZG 26. The remains of its crew, Oberfeldwebel Hans Tiepelt, the twenty-six-year-old pilot, and Unteroffizier Herbert Brosig, the wireless operator, aged twenty, were gathered from the yard and buried with Military Honours at Greenbank Cemetery, Bristol.

High above Bristol another German pilot was in trouble. Leutnant Joachim Koepsell of 3/ZG 26 was, like Hans Tiepelt

Filton Crew Hut. 504 Squadron at Filton, 1940. Left to right: Reggie Tongue, Murray Frisby, Tony Rook, Sgt H. Jones and Mike Rook. The swastika-bedecked fin was retrieved from the Bf 110 shot down by the squadron at Fishponds, Bristol, on 27 September 1940.

and the other pilots of I Gruppe, under orders to remain close to the aircraft of Erpr Gr 210 as they made their dive attack on the target, but as they approached Bristol things started to go seriously wrong. Koepsell, only twenty-one years old but a veteran of numerous air combats over Britain, remembers:

> It was wonderful, cloudless weather when we started from Cherbourg. As we approached the target and started our dive with the fighter-bombers we saw an English fighter squadron below, climbing towards us on an opposite course. We pulled up into a climbing turn to position for an attack on them, zooming to gain height quickly before starting down upon them, and at this point I had to change my position, moving from the right to the left of my formation. We continued our turn but as I looked around I saw, much to my surprise, that they were coming at us head-on at the same height. I believed our speed in the dive should have given us the better rate of climb, but the British fighters climbed faster than I anticipated. I had made a serious mistake and the enemy aircraft were quickly upon us.

Koepsell tried to pull his Bf 110 round in an attempt to get into a firing position and while still applying rudder and yawing he opened fire on a closing aircraft, having little hope of scoring a hit but, as he recalls:

> ... hoping that my tracer ammunition would have a psychological effect. Then everything seemed to happen very quickly. My aircraft was badly damaged in this first encounter – the starboard forward petrol tank caught fire, my windscreen was shot up and from my comrade Schmidt, in the back, I heard a rattle from his throat over the intercom. A feeling of great calm came over me; I was still alive but in my mirror I could see blood running down over my face. The state of my aircraft ruled out any chance of getting home or of even making a forced landing – the forward petrol tank was now burning fiercely while the large tank situated behind it could explode at any moment. Shortly before the attack I had pumped it dry, but I knew it still contained petrol vapour.

Leutnant Joachim Koepsell, shot down near Radstock, Somerset, 27 September 1940.

Koepsell continued:

I no longer had any communication with Schmidt in the rear cockpit, but I caught a sight of him slumped behind our inflatable rubber dinghy. With the certainty that a successful forced landing was no longer possible I decided to try to catapult him out of the rear cockpit, through the open canopy, by rapid pitching movements induced by fore and aft movements of the control column. I was hoping his straps were undone and that he would be able to open his parachute when he was clear of the aircraft. I then opened my own canopy roof exit, pulled myself up out of my seat and went out of the machine, pulling the ripcord after a delay of about five seconds.

I then found myself hanging from my parachute at a height of about 3,000 feet; looking down the English landscape looked unfamiliar but quite charming and from schooldays there came to mind a photograph I had seen in a geography book with the caption 'Typical English Parkland'. This idyllic memory was quickly gone as acute anxiety took over. A Spitfire came flying towards me and passed very close; I feared for my life as it appeared to be getting into a position to fire. I let my head hang to one side to imitate a dead airman, perhaps thereby sending away a possibly angry flier, for I was not shot at. Nor, indeed, was I shot at by a second British pilot who followed me in a like manner. I was not wearing the usual buff-coloured flying suit and perhaps my blue-grey combination was mistaken for RAF uniform.

As I drifted quietly down I became aware of hammer-like blows ringing out from below, as if from an English village smithy. Nearing the ground I could see that I was approaching some overhead wires so I pulled on my canopy lines to control my descent. This was partly successful, but in the end I finished up over a wood and finally landed in a tree. After crashing through some branches I came to rest some twelve to fifteen feet above the ground. Almost immediately I was greeted with a loud shout from someone, with orders to throw down my pistol. I did not comply with this request as I was too shaken at finding myself hanging in my parachute harness some distance above the ground. I was also not fully recovered from the shock of my recent encounter with the Spitfire.

Looking down I could see what I assumed was a Home Guard Officer.* He and his men were armed with a variety of guns, so I took it upon myself to explain to him that I was not hung in this fashion to become a sporting target of the English. To this the English officer responded dryly that neither was England a sporting target for German bombing practice. I conceded that he was, of course, right about that and asked him to release me quickly and take me to my aircraft and my comrade Schmidt. I was taken down, but my requests were refused. However, I later learned from the doctor with the unit that Unteroffizier Schmidt had left the machine all right but that he must have been knocked out or

---

* It was, in fact, an officer of the 1st Battalion Coldstream Guards.

killed before leaving. He landed with an unopened parachute close to the aircraft's dinghy. I also learned that my aircraft had exploded shortly before hitting the ground.

Joachim Koepsell owed his predicament to the marksmanship of Sergeant H.B.D. Jones of 504 Squadron who reported:

> I first engaged an enemy aircraft at 12,000 feet over Filton. I carried out a beam attack, firing a five seconds burst which brought smoke from its port engine. I then made a front attack on another aircraft, firing a three seconds burst this time, and the enemy aircraft turned over and dived straight down. It crashed to the south of Bristol, bursting into flames on impact.

The crash was again seen by many people including Mr Wilfred J. Candy, on whose farmland the Messerschmitt crashed. From Haydon Farm, situated near the Kilmersdon Road just outside Radstock, Somerset, Wilfred Candy had seen the German formation passing overhead en route to Yate. In addition to tending his farm, an important enough task in blockaded Britain, Candy was also a member of the Observer Corps. At 11.45 he stopped work outside his farmhouse to watch the returning aircraft, recognising them as Bf 110s, but instead of the near immaculate formation he had seen earlier he now saw scattered groups, chased and harried by British fighters.

His attention was drawn to one enemy aircraft in particular which, lower than the others, came whining down towards him with a British machine in close pursuit. As he watched the two aircraft come closer, heading straight towards his farmhouse, he could see that the Messerschmitt was trailing smoke. It began to pitch violently and then burst into flames. One of the crew was seen to bale out and shortly afterwards the aircraft appeared to break-up as it passed low over the farm. It hit the ground with a terrific rending of metal only 100 yards or so away from Wilfred Candy, beside the road leading over Haydon Hill. The wreckage burned fiercely, to the usual accompaniment of exploding ammunition and pyrotechnics.

As it broke-up over Haydon Farm the Bf 110's tail unit

became detached from the rear fuselage, a not uncommon occurrence with the twin engine Messerschmitt fighter, to land in a hillside clearing between the farmhouse and the Radstock-Frome railway line. Nearby lay the rubber dinghy and about half a mile distant, close to the Kilmersdon Colliery railway, Wilfred Candy found the body of Unteroffizier Johann Schmidt. The farmer could see that the German airman had been hit in the neck by machine-gun fire, but otherwise there was little to suggest that he had fallen from an aircraft with an unopened parachute.

Koepsell had landed a few miles distant at Terry Hill, near Mells. His captors were not members of the Home Guard as he imagined, but soldiers of the 1st Battalion of the Coldstream Guards stationed in nearby Mells. Another thing that Koepsell did not know was how very close he came to death when in the tree; some of the troops had been France prior to the evacuation from Dunkirk and being violently anti-German in consequence were angered by the German pilot's attitude. One soldier, with a bullet 'up the spout' – in the breech of his rifle – was about to shoot Koepsell, but he was restrained by colleagues.

An elderly couple, Mr and Mrs Sweet, also have memories of that day which they are unlikely to forget. Seeing Joachim Koepsell descending they hurried to where they expected him to land, taking an iron bar as a weapon, but they arrived to find the British soldiers already confronting the German officer. Upon reflection they were able to throw some light on the hammer-like blows mentioned by Koepsell – what he had heard was not a village smithy but the sound of a steam hammer in the Great Western Railway workshops at Mells Station.

Koepsell's aircraft was a Messerschmitt Bf 110 C4 that carried the markings U8+CL, but there is some doubt concerning the works number of this machine. German records give the number 3571, but this does not agree with that painted on the starboard fin – W.N.3352 – which was recovered from the clearing at Haydon Farm. German records could be incorrect, but another and more likely explanation is that the U8+CL was fitted with a fin taken from another Bf 110 being 'cannibalised' for spares. Another interesting feature is that the fin recovered at Radstock

Johann Schmidt in the rear cockpit of Joachim Koepsell's Bf 110.

A portion of the starboard fin of Bf 110 U8+CL shot down at Radstock, Somerset, 27 September 1940. The works number 3352 does not agree with the Werke Nummer given in German records (3571) and it is possible that a fin from a cannibalised aircraft was fitted. (see text)

bears traces of the red dope used to apply fabric patches to cover bullet holes in the metal skinning of aircraft. Joachim Koepsell can throw no light on the matter and does not recall that a fin of his aircraft was ever damaged or otherwise needed replacement.

XIII

Destroyers Destroyed

The rout of Erprobungsgruppe 210 and Zerstörergeschwader 26 continued unabated. Flight Lieutenant Tony Rook initially shared the rearguard 'weaver' duty with Pilot Officer Murray Frisby and was also among the first to engage, chasing an enemy aircraft from overhead Filton at 12,000 feet down to 4,000 feet. His victim eventually crashed into a hillside about sixteen miles north of Poole, but before it crashed he was joined in the affray by a Hurricane bearing the fuselage code markings US-M. This proved to be an aircraft of No 56 Squadron flown by Flying Officer Michael Constable-Maxwell.

Rook's cousin, Pilot Officer Mike Rook, was involved in two separate combats; the first, over Filton at 12,000 feet with AA shells bursting all around him, proved inconclusive, but his second attack produced flames from both engines of a Bf 110 that went into a vertical dive to crash to the south of Cerne Abbas.

Another pilot of No 504 Squadron who first went into action over Filton and finished up pursuing his victim out over the South Coast was Sergeant Charlton Haw, better known to his squadron colleagues as 'Wag'. He fired a long burst of ten seconds into a Bf 110 flying at 14,000 feet which immediately caught fire and went into the sea in a spin.

By mid-day the first returning Hurricanes of 504 Squadron had landed back at Filton where the score was eagerly added up by the ground crews who had witnessed much of the action. To their delight the claims indicated five destroyed with three 'probables'. Ten of the squadron's twelve Hurricanes returned to Filton while Sergeant Mike Bush landed at Weston Airport, short of fuel, and Sergeant Haw forced landed at Axminster. Haw returned to Filton that evening and upon arrival registered his claim of another enemy aircraft destroyed, bringing the

squadron's total to six. There was good cause for celebration
that night, as in the messes at Warmwell, Boscombe Down and
Middle Wallop. At Cherbourg, on the other hand, there was
little to celebrate.

All four complete squadrons and the single section of No 238
Squadron had made contact with and engaged the enemy. The
two Hurricanes of 238, flown by Pilot Officer Urwin-Mann and
Sergeant Jeka had encountered groups of returning Bf 110s,
Urwin-Mann damaging one and Jeka, in the company of some
Spitfires of 609 Squadron, destroying another.

The Hurricanes of No 56 Squadron were also in action to the
south of Bristol against returning aircraft, Pilot Officer Marston
destroying one Bf 110 and damaging another, Pilot Officer
Higginson claiming one damaged and Pilot Officer MacKenzie
claiming damage to what he thought was a Dornier. Michael
Constable-Maxwell also claimed a Dornier destroyed but, as
previously mentioned, this was unquestionably a Bf 110.

The Spitfires of 152 Squadron encountered the enemy
formations returning south-east at high speed and became
engaged in a running battle from the Bristol area to the south
coast and beyond. In the coastal region they were themselves
attacked by the Bf 109s sent over to cover the withdrawal of Erpr
Gr 210 and its long-range escort.

All 152 Squadron's Combat Reports mention Ju 88s as well as
Bf 109s and 110s, but aircraft recognition problems were again
to blame. Pilot Officers Cox and Inness became involved with
the Bf 109s which, they reported, had yellow painted spinners
and upper engine cowlings; Inness claimed the destruction of
one at 25,000 feet west of Yeovil, while Cox claimed a Bf 110.
Over the south coast Cox saw a Bf 109 rapidly closing in behind
his Number Two, Pilot Officer Bayles, who was himself climbing
after some more Bf 109s heading out to sea. Bayles's port wing
was hit by cannon fire, but he landed safely, despite the presence
of a cannon shell nose in one of his tyres. Prior to this
entanglement with the Bf 109s Bayles had damaged a Bf 110.

Pilot Officers Holmes and Hall of 152 Squadron followed an
already damaged Bf 110 and saw it crash in a field. Holmes was
unsuccessful in his bid to shoot down several other aircraft that

Playful NCOs of 504 Squadron at Filton, 1940. Left to right: Sergeants Jones, Spencer, Haywood and Haw.

Filton Incident. Soft ground resulted in this taxying accident to Hurricane TM:Q at Filton, 1940.

he engaged, but Hall climbed back up to 15,000 feet and chased another Bf 110, causing it to emit white smoke or glycol coolant from its port engine. When last seen it was diving towards the sea.

A Bf 110 attacked by Flight Lieutenant Thomas of the same squadron took evasive action in the form of steep climbing and diving turns, but Thomas closed to 150 yards and poured all his ammunition into it. The port engine of the enemy aircraft was emitting black smoke when the British pilot was obliged to break away with a Bf 109 on his tail. Thomas's Number Two, Pilot Officer Watson, attacked one enemy aircraft in the Southampton area and when last seen it was trailing smoke and diving towards the sea off the Isle of Wight; not content with this Watson climbed back to 15,000 feet where he fired at a Bf 110 which streamed glycol from its starboard engine as it dived away. The British pilot followed it, firing intermittent bursts, and at about 1,000 feet the enemy machine exploded and crashed into a wood to the south-west of Poole Harbour.

Yet another Bf 110 fell to the guns of Pilot Officer Williams, also of 152 Squadron. After first attempting evasive manoeuvres the German pilot tried to escape by relying on speed alone, but as it headed south Dudley Williams continued to attack from astern and both engines of the 110, already leaving thin trails of smoke, suddenly emitted dense white smoke and went into a steep dive. Williams followed, keeping up his attack with short bursts of fire, until he finally saw his opponent crash on land near Lulworth Cove.

The twelve Spitfires of No 609 Squadron led by Pilot Officer Miller following the R/T failures suffered by the two Flight Commanders, came upon about fifteen Bf 110s that had formed a defensive circle south of Blandford Forum. As the Spitfires approached at high speed one of the Bf 110s broke out of the circle and turned towards the British fighters. Seconds later the Messerschmitt and the Spitfire flown by Miller collided. The Spitfire blew up immediately, killing its pilot, and the Bf 110 went down on fire and out of control with Gefreiter Emil Lidtke, the wireless operator, dead in the rear cockpit. Almost miraculously Gefreiter Georg Jackstedt, the Bf 110's pilot, managed to get free to descend by parachute.

The remains of Miller's Spitfire and Jackstedt's Bf 110 were seen to crash to the ground by Mr Philip Tory, then farming at Piddlehinton, Dorset. The collision had occurred at 24,000 feet and little wreckage was recognisable when it landed, the German machine being on fire and breaking up as it fell. Tory set off towards the place where the main part of the wreckage crashed to earth and on the way passed an engine that had landed in a field some distance from where most of the wreckage lay in a hedge bordering Doles Ash Farm and Bellamy's Farm, near Piddletrenthide. The latter was farmed in those days by the late Mr Ralph Wightman, the well-known West Country broadcaster and TV personality of later years.

When Philip Tory arrived at the remains of the Messerschmitt it was burning, with the wireless operator still in the rear cockpit. The farmer could see the airman's extensive head wounds as he lay slumped in his seat amid the smoke and flames. Ralph Wightman recalled that when the body was removed from the wreckage it was left in full view for some hours before someone covered it with a sheet. Later a dispute arose over the burial, one report indicating that the local clergy refused to bury the body; apparently the dead airman was eventually buried beside the hedgerow where he fell. The grave, it was said, was unmarked for some time but one day a cross materialised and flowers appeared on the grave from time to time, placed there by an unknown person. Ralph Wightman, living some five miles distant at the time, had no recollection of the burial at the crash site, but remembered a dispute between the local Church or Parish Council and the War Office concerning payment for the burial and where this should take place. As Philip Tory remarked, 'All England was a battlefield in those days' and it did not seem inappropriate to bury the German where he fell, but eventually Lidtke was laid to rest in Brookwood Military Cemetery, Surrey.

Gefreiter Georg Jackstedt, although wounded, managed to parachute to safety. Upon landing he was met by a nineteen-year-old youth named Chambers who ran some three miles to reach him. Jackstedt, who landed in a field minus his boots, could speak a little English and rather surprisingly sought confirmation from his captor that he had landed in England. He was clearly in a state of shock. He also asked for news of his colleague and while the young Englishman, later to become well known as a photographer in Weymouth, helped him to remove his parachute harness the airman spoke of his wife and three children living in Königsberg. Chambers recalled that the German was unarmed. When offered some lemonade by one of the crowd that soon gathered he at first seemed hesitant, but later accepted. Shortly afterwards he was taken away by the police.

Not far distant, at Chesilbourne, the body of Mick Miller was found in the wreckage of his Spitfire. Since joining the squadron at Northolt on 26th June, Miller had accounted for three enemy aircraft and had shared in the destruction of two more. He was also credited with a 'probable' and two enemy aircraft damaged.

Five more Bf 110s and a Bf 109 were credited to No 609 Squadron, the twin-engined fighters being claimed by Flying Officer John Dundas, Pilot Officers John Bisdee and David Crook (shared), Pilot Officer M.E. Staples and Pilot Officer Noel le C. Agazarian. The Bf 109 was claimed by Flying Officer T.H.T. Forshaw.

Noel Agazarian was somewhat disgruntled when he was attacked by some Hurricanes while he himself was in pursuit of twelve Bf 109s over Portland at 23,000 feet; in consequence his section was forced to break up, but reforming again they met up with another group of the enemy and he shot down a Bf 110 which crashed into the sea twenty-five miles south of Portland Bill.*

Following their many successes the pilots of 609 Squadron received messages of congratulation from the Secretary of State for Air, Sir Archibald Sinclair, and from Air Chief Marshal Dowding. Sir Stanley White of the Bristol Aeroplane Company expressed his thanks, too, for in his view the squadron's contribution 'undoubtedly saved the factory from serious

---

* The Spitfire flown by Pilot Officer Agazarian in both the actions described in this book survived the war and is on permanent display in the Imperial War Museum at Lambeth, London.

damage and heartened and encouraged all the factory employees'. He was unaware, of course, that Filton was not the intended target, but his comments held good for his employees and were equally applicable to the true objective at Yate.

In due course the claims of the British squadrons were totalled and eventually after much checking by squadron intelligence officers, the destruction of nineteen German aircraft was agreed.

Across the Channel a similar inquisition found that ten British fighters had been destroyed. The Bf 109s of II/JG 2, sweeping ahead of the main force, had made no contact with British fighters and neither lost any aircraft nor made any claims. I and III Gruppen of JG 2, whose Bf 109s covered the withdrawal of the Bf 110s, reported combats with single Spitfires near Poole and Christchurch, claiming three Spitfires destroyed. One each were claimed by Hauptmann Helmut Wick and Oberfeldwebel Machold, these alleged 'kills' bringing the former's total number of victories to 31 and Machold's to 22.

The seven Bf 109s of JG 53 which joined forces with JG 2 to cover the retreat, reported an action with 25-30 Spitfires north-west of the Isle of Wight at 24,000 feet, but they made no claims and suffered no loss to themselves. A pilot of Erpr Gr 210 claimed the destruction of a Hurricane, but the highest number of victories – four Hurricanes and two Spitfires – went to the pilots of ZG 26.

So much for the claims, but for both sides the reality was rather different. RAF Squadron records and Fighter Command Combat and Casualty returns show that only one British fighter was totally destroyed (Category 3), this being Spitfire X4107 that was in collision with the Bf 110 over Dorset. Its pilot, Pilot Officer Miller of No 609 Squadron, was the only British casualty. Another fighter, Hurricane P3415 of 504 Squadron, was damaged in a forced landing, but no other aircraft or pilots were lost.

The British figures of nineteen German aircraft destroyed, one probably destroyed, and eleven damaged, were also in error, but not as wildly inaccurate as the German claim. In fact only ten German aircraft were lost, but four of these belonged to Erpr Gr

210 and represented 40% of the attacking fighter-bomber force. Worse, among this unit's casualties were the *Gruppenkommandeur*, Hauptmann Martin Lutz, and the *Staffelkapitän* of 2 Staffel, Oberleutnant Wilhelm Rössiger.

Three of the German losses – the Bf 110s of ZG 26 that crashed at Fishponds (Bristol), Radstock, and Piddletrenthide in Dorset – can be positively credited to the British pilots responsible and these incidents have been described at some length. Other crashed German aircraft, however, are not so easily linked in view of the many claims submitted by the British pilots.

It seems fairly certain, however, that Hauptmann Lutz's aircraft was hit by Frisby of 504 Squadron over Bristol, but it was probably also attacked later by other aircraft. The attack leader's aircraft crashed at Bussey Stool Farm, Cranbourne Chase, some five miles south-east of Shaftesbury, and both Lutz and his wireless operator, Unteroffizier Anton Schön, were killed, their Bf 110 hitting some trees at high speed before it struck the ground. Martin Lutz had previously flown in the Spanish Civil War with the Condor Legion and later served as a *Staffelkapitän* with a *Zerstörer* unit, I/ZG 1 before joining 1/Erpr Gr 210. He was posthumously awarded the *Ritterkreuz* on 1st October. It is likely, but by no means certain, that the German fighter-bomber leader was finally shot down by Flight Lieutenant A.H. Rook of 504 Squadron, joined by Flying Officer M.H. Constable-Maxwell of 56 Squadron.

Another Bf 110 came to grief at The Beeches, near Iwerne Minster, Dorset, in a field alongside the A 350 road. Its pilot, Feldwebel Fritz Ebner, made a good belly landing, his aircraft being only slightly damaged by a small number of hits, mostly in the engines. Ebner was only slightly hurt and was taken into military custody at Shroton, but his gunner, Gefreiter Werner Zwick, was taken to Shaftesbury Hospital, seriously wounded. They and their aircraft, which carried the markings S9+DU, belonged to 2/Erpr Gr 210.

Pilot Officer Watson of 152 Squadron claimed an enemy aircraft that crashed into a wood south-west of Poole Harbour and it seems most likely that this was the 3U+IM, a Bf 110 of

4/ZG 26 that crashed near Arne, Wareham, killing both crew members. One report states that this aircraft was diving with one engine on fire, following an attack by a Spitfire, when it was further hit by AA fire and disintegrated.

Not far from Wareham, at Kimmeridge, another two Bf 110s came down. One was totally destroyed when it dived into the ground, making a deep crater and killing its crew. Little was found to identify this aircraft or its crew, but almost certainly it was the 3U+BD (crewed by Oberleutnant Hans Barschel and Unteroffizier Klose) that, according to German records, failed to return from this mission. Nearby, only a mile south-west of Kimmeridge Church, Unteroffizier Fritz Schupp of III/ZG 26 successfully forced landed his 3U+DS, little damaged apart from its port engine. Schupp stated that he was first attacked by two Spitfires that attacked from out of the sun and then came at him one from each side. This happened to the east of Portland, as the German formation was on its way to Bristol at 21,000 feet. Schupp's port engine was disabled and caught fire, but neither he nor his wireless operator, Gefreiter Karl Nechwatal, were hurt. They were taken prisoner and initially detained at the HQ of the 4th East Yorks Regiment at Kimmeridge.

Schupp's aircraft was examined by officers of A.I. 1(g) Branch who reported that both rudders and wings showed signs of 0·303 inch strikes and that the fuel system was damaged. It carried standard armament but no armour plate. Its individual identification letter 'D' took the form of a thin black letter broadly outlined in white. It also carried two yellow bars on its rudders and tailplane, had dark green spinners with a red ring around them, and sported three 'Kill' bars denoting victories over RAF aircraft.

Finally, two Bf 110s of Erpr Gr 210 are believed to have crashed into the sea off the Dorset coast. One was the S9+JH of 1 Staffel, crewed by Leutnant Gerhard Schmidt and Feldwebel Gerhard Richter. The bodies of both men were recovered and they were buried at Brookwood Military Cemetery.

The other aircraft was the S9+GK flown by 2 Staffel's *Kapitän*, Oberleutnant Wilhelm Rössiger. German reports state that this aircraft was seen to dive into the sea and both Rössiger and his

Oberleutnant Wilhelm Rössiger, Staffelkapitän of 2/Erpr
Gr 210. Killed during the attack on Yate, 27 September
1940.

wireless operator, Oberfeldwebel Hans Marx, are still officially listed as missing, their bodies having never been found. Rössiger, aged twenty-six, was posthumously awarded the *Ritterkreuz* on the same day as his *Gruppenkommandeur*, Martin Lutz. The citation credited both men with long operational careers, culminating with a destructive attack on an aircraft factory on the south coast. This presumably referred to the attack on the Supermarine factory at Woolston, Southampton, on 24th September, when, in fact, little serious damage was caused but many people died when an air raid shelter was hit.

Daily Summary No 59, issued by the Bristol office of the Regional Commissioner, South-West Region Civil Defence, states quite simply; 'Any ill effects on public morale caused by the raid on 25.9.40 were more than offset by the defeat and dispersal of the raiders before they reached their objective on 27.9.40.' And this one sentence precisely summarises the situation.

Of the two attacks the first, by a large formation of slow bombers escorted by an inadequate number of twin-engined fighters, looked much less likely to succeed than the second, attempted by a compact force of fast fighter-bombers supported by an escort of substantial proportions. Yet, contrary to this expectation, the first was a qualified success, the second surely one of the most disastrous and totally ineffective operations undertaken by the Luftwaffe in World War Two.

The disastrous operation of 27th September was virtually the swan song of the Bf 110 over Britain, the final writing on the wall for the 110-equipped *Zerstörer* and fighter-bomber Gruppen. Later, in less demanding theatres of war and when employed as a night fighter in the defence of the Reich, the twin-engined Messerschmitt was to re-assert itself, but its days over Britain were numbered. Numbered, too, were the days of the large, escorted daylight attacks. The onset of cloudy late autumn weather and the continued ascendency of Royal Air Force fighters over the German long-range escort fighters finally sounded the death knell of the daylight precision bomber attack at *Geschwader* strength. Finely balanced for so long, the scales tipped at last in favour of the defenders, at least during the hours of daylight. At night the tilt reversed – but that is another part of the history of the air war over Britain.

XIV

Postscript

No account of the operations of 25th and 27th September 1940 would be complete without relating something of the subsequent fate of some of the participants. As one would expect, many of the airmen were to lose their lives in the long, hard struggle that still lay ahead, but a surprisingly large number survived.

H.S. Darley, in command of No 609 Squadron and then a twenty-seven-year-old Regular officer, was one who survived the war, winning the Distinguished Service Order in the process. Better known as 'George' he was held in the highest esteem by all who served under him, having taken over the command of the squadron when morale was at a low ebb and thoroughly rejuvenating it. As a Group Captain in the post-war air force he at one time commanded RAF Cranfield. Keith Ogilvie, one of his pilots and a Canadian from Ottawa, also survived; after the award of the Distinguished Flying Cross he was shot down over France and taken prisoner, but returned safely after the war.

John Dundas, a pre-war journalist, was less fortunate. In late November 1940 he was lost over the Isle of Wight after, it is believed, shooting down the German ace Major Helmut Wick. It appears he was himself then shot down by Wick's wingman. At the time Wick, who is known to have flown in the attack of 27th September, was credited with 56 combat victories. David Crook of 609 Squadron, also in action on the 27th and well-known as the author of *Spitfire Pilot*, was also killed later on.

Two of the three pilots of No 601 Squadron in action on the 25th were subsequently to lose their lives, only A.J.H. Aldwinkle surviving. Howard Mayers' death was a cruel twist of fate; shot down and captured in the Middle East in 1942, he was killed when the German transport aircraft taking him to Italy was shot down by a Spitfire.

Of the pilots of No 152 Squadron, F.H. Holmes, J. McBean Christie and Eric Marrs were killed, in addition to Kenneth Holland who died in the crash at Woolverton on 25th September.

The twelve pilots of 238 Squadron seem to have been more fortunate, all of them surviving so far as can be determined. Jack Urwin-Mann went on to shoot down at least twelve enemy aircraft while serving in the United Kingdom, Malta and the Middle East and was awarded the Distinguished Service Order, the Distinguished Flying Cross and Bar. After the war he commanded No 1 Squadron for a time, flying Meteor jet fighters.

Five pilots of No 56 Squadron are known to have died in action and the same number of pilots of 504 Squadron were lost including Murray Frisby, whose head-on attack on the leader of the German formation broke up the raid of 27th September. Michael Rook, responsible for the destruction of the Bf 110 at Cerne Abbas, was also killed, as was H.D.B. Jones, the pilot who shot down Joachim Koepsell at Radstock. Charlton 'Wag' Haw of the same squadron later went to Russia with an RAF contingent and was awarded the Order of Lenin. He was commissioned upon his return and commanded No 611 Squadron in 1943, receiving the DFC the following year. After the war he remained in the Service. Barrington Royce, who led the squadron on the 27th in the absence of its commanding officer, rose to the rank of Group Captain. In retirement he lived in his native Nottinghamshire but—and this is particularly sad to relate in view of his major contribution—he died just prior to the publication of the first edition of this book. His brother Michael, who shot down the Bf 110 over Bristol, also survived the war and now resides in the Isle of Wight. John Sample, their squadron commander in September 1940, later took over the command of No. 137 Squadron and was killed in a Whirlwind twin-engined fighter of that unit in October 1941.

Douglas Wingrove, formerly of RAF Yatesbury, was later commissioned and also returned home after the war, as did Kenneth Grater of the 76th HAA Regiment, and ex-Sergeant Major Richards. Thomas Meadway, involved with the He 111 crash at Woolverton, subsequently joined the army, returning as a major at the end of hostilities. He retired from business some years ago but is still living in the area. Others connected with the capture of German airmen who survived into the seventies include 'Chubby' Ball, Mr L.W. Trew, Mr and Mrs Theo Janku, Mrs Marshallsay and Philip Tory. Mr Wilfred Candy and his wife now live in retirement in Bath, while Mr and Mrs Sweet continue to live near Radstock. Ralph Wightman, of rich West Country accent fame, unfortunately died some years ago, as many of his former BBC listeners will know.

Unlike their opposite numbers in the RAF, the German airmen of World War Two knew no such thing as an operational tour – once employed on operations they so continued until death, serious injury, captivity, or transfer to a staff appointment brought relief. As a result many members of KG 55, ZG 26 and Erpr Gr 210 did not live to see the end of the war. One who did, of course, was Friedrich Kless, the leader of the attack of 25th September and the writer of the introduction to this book. The day after the Filton attack he was engaged in another large scale operation against the Spitfire factory at Woolston, Southampton, and shortly afterwards he was awarded the coveted *Ritterkreuz*. In November 1940 he took up a staff appointment at V Fliegerkorps headquarters and in April 1941 moved to the Lublin area in preparation for the invasion of Russia. He served in that campaign until November, when he returned to Brussels in connection with bomber operations over Britain. From January 1942 until the end of the war he again served on the Eastern Front, at first as a Staff Officer in the Crimea and then with Luftflottenkommando Ost on the Centre Sector of the front. An expert on East European and Russian affairs, 'Fritz' Kless was appointed Chief of the General Staff with Luftflottenkommando 6 in February 1943 and at the end of the war, with the rank of Generalmajor, he was taken prisoner by the US Army and interned at Dachau. At the end of 1947 he was released from captivity and entered a career in business management. He retired some years ago and now lives happily in his native Bavaria.

Willi Antrup also survived the war and now lives in retirement, also in southern Bavaria. He received the Knight's

Battle Survivor. Supermarine Spitfire Mk IA R6915, flown by Pilot Officer Noel Agazarian on 25th and 27th September 1940, now on permanent display at the Imperial War Museum, London.

Cross in 1942 and later became *Kommandeur* of III/KG 55. In 1943 he was appointed *Kommodore* of the entire *Geschwader* and in 1944, after completing the incredible total of more than 500 operational flights, was awarded the Knight's Cross with Oak Leaves. Following his remarkable wartime career Antrup served in the post-war Bundeswehr, retiring in 1968 with the rank of Brigadegeneral.

Dr Ernst Kühl, like Antrup destined to become a *Kommodore* of KG 55, was appointed Lufttransportführer Stalingrad in 1942, responsible for all air transport operations in support of the beleaguered German garrison. A truly remarkable man, he was an artillery officer in World War One, was forty-four years old when he learned to fly, and was fifty-two when he flew in the attack on Filton. Shortly after this operation he was shot down into the English Channel and was rescued by the German air/sea rescue organisation after thirty-six hours adrift in a rubber dinghy. He resumed flying duties and when fifty-seven years old completed his 315th operational flight, by then an *Oberst* and a holder of the Knight's Cross with Oak Leaves. He died in 1972, shortly before his eighty-fourth birthday.

During the winter of 1940/1941 Kampfgeschwader 55 was engaged in the Night Blitz against British industrial towns and ports. Losses were at a lower level than during the Battle of Britain, but many of the airmen that took part in the action of 25th September against Filton were to lose their lives when the unit moved to the Eastern Front. Among those who survived was Heinz Höfer, a later *Kommandeur* of II/KG 55 and yet another recipient of the Knight's Cross with Oak Leaves. Werner Oberländer also went to Russia with KG 55 in 1941, became a holder of the *Ritterkreuz* but was seriously wounded later on.

Two members of KG 55 who did not go east, however, were Johannes Speck von Sternberg and Martin Reiser. The latter was shot down during the last major night attack on London on 10th May 1941 and taken prisoner. A kind and spritely gentleman to the end, he died in 1980 at the age of 82. When shot down he was a *Leutnant* and the *Kommandant* of his own aircraft. By a strange coincidence that very same night his former pilot and *Staffelkapitän*, Speck von Sternberg, was shot down and killed near Birmingham.

Of the former German airmen shot down and taken prisoner during the two attacks all returned to Germany eventually. Walter Scherer's internment in Canada was somewhat unusual for while a prisoner of war he married by proxy his fiancée Grete, then living in Mannheim. They were eventually reunited after some six years apart and settled down to a more normal married life, building up a successful business in the aftermath of a defeated and divided Germany. The happy partnership continued until 1969 when a heart attack brought about the death of the former *Zerstörer* pilot at the early age of 54.

While a POW Karl Gerdsmeier became seriously ill and was repatriated from Canada in May 1944, but he recovered to take up a normal life as a civilian. His comrades Georg Engel and Karl Geib did not return to Germany until released in 1947. Geib is now a senior official in a West German government department while Engel, who was taken from the Clevedon Cottage Hosptial to the Royal Herbert Hospital in Woolwich before transfer to a normal POW camp, is in business. The observer in their crew, Alfred Narres, also returned to Germany to become a police officer and is now living in the Ruhr area. None of the crew have had recent contact with their former pilot and *Kommandant*, Gottfried Weigel, but it is known that he too returned safely after the war.

Other former members of KG 55 who survived into recent times include Helmut Kindor, Kurt Schraps, Karl Köthke, Fritz Jürges (who, in 1977, made a return trip to Studland to see again the place where he was taken prisoner in 1940), and Rudolf Weisbach. Otto Müller, the young gunner in the Heinkel that crashed at Studland, is now with the criminal police at Saarbrüken, where he also coaches an ice hockey team. For more than twenty years he was an investigator into Nazi war crimes for the German authorities at Ludwigsburg. His former *Staffelkapitän*, Karl Köthke, lives in happy retirement growing flowers in his garden near Bremen.

Another recent visitor to England was Joachim Koepsell, holidaying with his wife and four sons and visiting Radstock to renew his acquaintanceship with the 'typical English parkland' he had first seen as he descended by parachute on 27th September 1940. A less 'typical, arrogant Nazi', as he was once called by his captors, it would be difficult to imagine, yet this was the man who so nearly met his end at the hands of irate British soldiers who themselves had suffered much at Dunkirk. Such is war; through the ages it has seen the worst examples of man's inhumanity to man strangely paralleled by examples of man at his best, and never was this more apparent than during the Second World War. Nevertheless, no one who survived it would wish for the experience again.

Appendix 1

KAMPFGESCHWADER 55 – ORGANISATION & SENIOR OFFICERS
25 September 1940

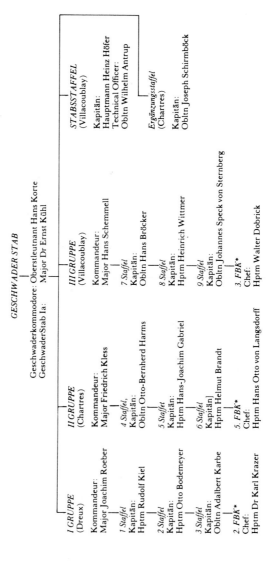

GESCHWADER STAB

Geschwaderkommodore: Oberstleutnant Hans Korte
GeschwaderStab Ia: Major Dr Ernst Kühl

STABSSTAFFEL
(Villacoublay)

Kapitän:
Hauptmann Heinz Höfer
Technical Officer:
Obltn Wilhelm Antrup

Ergänzungsstaffel
(Chartres)

Kapitän:
Obltn Joseph Schirmböck

III GRUPPE
(Villacoublay)

Kommandeur:
Major Hans Schemmell

7 Staffel
Kapitän:
Obltn Hans Bröcker

8 Staffel
Kapitän:
Hptm Heinrich Wittmer

9 Staffel
Kapitän:
Obltn Johannes Speck von Sternberg

3. FBK*
Chef:
Hptm Walter Dobrick

II GRUPPE
(Chartres)

Kommandeur:
Major Friedrich Kless

4 Staffel
Kapitän:
Obltn Otto-Bernherd Harms

5 Staffel
Kapitän:
Hptm Hans-Joachim Gabriel

6 Staffel
Kapitän]
Hptm Helmut Brandt

5. FBK*
Chef:
Hptm Hans Otto von Langsdorff

I GRUPPE
(Dreux)

Kommandeur:
Major Joachim Roeber

1 Staffel
Kapitän:
Hptm Rudolf Kiel

2 Staffel
Kapitän:
Hptm Otto Bodemeyer

3 Staffel
Kapitän:
Obltn Adalbert Karbe

2. FBK*
Chef:
Hptm Dr Karl Krazer

* 2, 3 and 5 Flughafenbetriebskompanien attached to KG 55 for aircraft maintenance and ground support

Appendix 2

ORDER OF BATTLE, No. 10 GROUP FIGHTER COMMAND
25 September 1940

Air Officer Commanding: Air Vice-Marshal Sir Christopher Quintin Brand.
Headquarters: Rudloe Manor, Box, Wiltshire.

Filton Sector:
87 Squadron, Hurricanes (LK), Exeter (one Flight) Bibury (one Flight)
(Sq Ldr R.S. Mills)

601 Squadron, Hurricanes (UF), Exeter
(Sq Ldr Sir A.P. Hope)

Pembrey Sector:
79 Squadron, Hurricanes (NV), Pembrey
(Sq Ldr J.E. Heyworth)

Middle Wallop Sector:
152 Squadron, Spitfires (UM), Warmwell
(Sq Ldr P.K. Devitt)

238 Squadron, Hurricanes (VK), Middle Wallop
(Sq Ldr H.A. Fenton)

609 (West Riding) Squadron, Spitfires (PR), Middle Wallop
(Sq Ldr H.S. Darley)

56 Squadron, Hurricanes (US), Boscombe Down
(Sq Ldr H.M. Pinfold)

604 (County of Middlesex) Squadron, Blenheims (NG), Middle Wallop (Night fighters)
(Sq Ldr M.F. Anderson)

St Eval Sector:
247 Squadron, Gladiators (HP), Roborough (one Flight)
(Flt Lt H.A. Chater)

234 Squadron, Spitfires (AZ), St Eval
(Sq Ldr J.S. O'Brien)

Note: Squadron code lettering in parenthesis after aircraft type.

Appendix 3

No 609 (West Riding) Squadron (Vickers Supermarine Spitfire Mk IA)

Plt Off A.K. Ogilvie (Canada)	N3280
Sgt J. Hughes Rees +	L1008
Plt Off R.F.G Miller + (Australia)	X4107
Sgt A.N. Feary +	X4234
Plt Off M.E. Staples +	L1096
Flg Off J.C. Newbury	R6691
Flg Off J.C. Dundas +	X4472
Sq Ldr H.S. Darley	R6979
Flt Lt J.H.G. McArthur	X4165
Plt Off N. le C. Agazarian +	R6915
Plt Off J. Curchin +	R6699
Flg Off Ostaszewski (Poland)	N3288
Flg Off T.H.T. Forshaw	X4471
Flg Off T. Nowierski (Poland)	N3223

No 601 (County of London) Squadron (Hawker Hurricane Mk I)
(Red Section only)

Flg Off H.C. Mayers +	R4218
Plt Off A.J.H. Aldwinkle	P3675
Flg Off J.S. Jankiewicz + (Poland)	V6666

No 152 Squadron (Vickers Supermarine Spitfire Mk IA)*

Flt Lt D.P.A. Boitel-Gill +	–
Plt Off R.F. Inness	–
Plt Off C.S. Cox	–
Plt Off F.H. Holmes +	–
Sgt R. Wolton	–
Plt Off R.M.D. Hall	–
Sq Ldr P.K. Devitt	–
Sgt K.C. Holland + (Australia)	–
Plt Off D.W. Williams	–
Sgt J. McBean Christie +	–
Plt Off T.N. Bayles	–
Plt Off E.S. Marrs +	–

No 238 Squadron (Hawker Hurricane Mk I)

Sq Ldr H.A. Fenton	P2920
Plt Off V.C. Simmonds	P3178
Plt Off D.S. Harrison	P3222
Plt Off J.R. Urwin-Mann (Canada)	P4232
Sgt V. Horsky (Czechoslovakia)	V6777
Plt Off A.R. Kings	V6792
Sgt L.G. Batt	V6727
Sgt J. Kucera (Czechoslovakia)	N2546
Sgt F.A. Sibley	R2681
Sgt R. Little	P3836
Plt Off W. Rozycki (Poland)	P3618
Plt Off J.S. Wigglesworth	P3767

+ Killed in action or on active service during the war.

* Aircraft serial numbers are not shown in 152 Squadron records.

Appendix 4

RAF COMBAT CLAIMS – DEFENCE OF FILTON
25 September, 1940

Squadron	Destroyed	Probably Destroyed	Damaged
No 609	1 Do 215	3 Do 17	1 Do 215
	1 Bf 110	1 Bf 110	
	2 He 111	1 unidentified	
	2 unidentified		
No 601	2 Bf 110		1 Bf 110
No 152	3 Ju 88		2 He 111
	1 Do 17 or Bf 110		1 Bf 110
	½ He 111 (shared)		
No 238	6 He 111		2 He 111
Totals:	18½	5	7

Note: The claims shown here are those recorded in the Squadrons' Operations Record Books and are not verified. Aircraft other than Bf 110s and He 111s are wrongly identified as only German aircraft of these types were involved.

Appendix 5

RAF CASUALTIES – DEFENCE OF FILTON
25 September, 1940

Aircraft type and Serial No.	Squadron	Pilot	Time and Place
Spitfire Mk.IA (Category 1)	152	Plt.Off. G.J. Cox (uninjured)	1145 hrs. Damaged near Yeovil; returned to Warmwell.
Spitfire Mk.IA (Category 1)	152	Plt.Off. E.S. Marrs (uninjured)	1145 hrs. Damaged near Bristol; returned to Warmwell.
Spitfire Mk.IA L1008 (Category 2)	609	Sgt. J. Hughes Rees (uninjured)	1150 hrs. Forced landed in a field near Glastonbury, Somerset.
Spitfire Mk.IA (Category 3)	152	Sq.Ldr. P.K. Devitt (uninjured)	1155 hrs. Forced landed in a field near Newton St. Loe, Somerset.
Spitfire Mk.IA (Category 3)	152	Sgt. K.C. Holland (killed)	1200 hrs. Crashed in a field at Woolverton, Somerset, and totally destroyed.
Hurricane Mk.I P3222 (Category 1)	238	Sgt. D.S. Harrison (uninjured)	1205 hrs. Forced landed in a field between Frome and Radstock, Somerset. Slight damage only and took off later.
Hurricane Mk.I R2681* (Category 3)	238	Sgt. F.A. Sibley (uninjured)	1205 hrs. Destroyed in an attempted forced landing at Charmy Down, Somerset.

Note: Category 1 damage – slight, repairable by unit.
  Category 2 damage – moderate, repairable on site with assistance from manufacturer or Maintenance Unit.
  Category 3 damage – Written off, beyond repair.

* One entry in No 238 Squadron records states that Hurricane N2597 was destroyed in this incident. Another entry states R2681.

Appendix 6

GERMAN CASUALTIES – ATTACK ON FILTON
25 September, 1940

1. 1150 hrs. Racecourse Farm, Failand, near Bristol. Shot down by A.A. fire.
   He 111 P (W.Nr.2126), G1+DN of 5./K.G.55
   - (F)   Obltn. Gottfried Weigel (u) (Paramaribo, Dutch Guiana, 27.8.1914)
   - (B)   Ofw. Alfred Narres   (u) (Essen, 20.11.1910)
   - (Bf) Fw. Georg Engel   (w)(Gross-Gerau, 2.6.1913)
   - (Bm) Uffz. Karl Gerdsmeier   (u) (Kleinenbrennen, 15.10.1914)
   - (Bs) Gefr. Karl Geib   (u) (Miesenback, 31.12.1919)

2. 1200 hrs. Church Farm, Woolverton, Somerset. Shot down by fighters.
   He 111 P (W.Nr.1525), G1+EP of 6./K.G.55
   - (F)   Hptm. Helmut Brandt
           (Staffelkapitän)   (w)(Magdeburg, 2.1.1907)
   - (B)   Ofw. Günter Wittkamp (d) (Hamburg, 4.12.1916)
   - (Bf) Ofw. Rudolf Kirchoff (d) (Braunschweig, 19.12.1911)
   - (Bm) Uffz. Hans-Fritz Mertz (d) (Auerheim, 28.4.1918)
   - (Bs) Gefr. Rudolf Beck   (d) (Murau, 10.6.1920)

3. 1200 hrs. Well Bottom, near Boyton, Wilts. Shot down by fighter action.
   Bf 110 C4 (W.Nr.3591), 3U+GS of 8./Z.G.26
   - (F)   Fw. Walter Scherer   (w)(14.5.1915)
   - (Bf) Gefr. Heinz
           Schumacher   (d)

4. 1209 hrs. Westminster Road, Branksome Park, Poole, Dorset. Shot down by fighters.
   He 111 P (W.Nr.2803), G1+LR of 7./K.G.55
   - (F)   Obltn. Hans Bröcker
           (Staffelkapitän)   (d) (Gr.Rhüden, 26.5.1911)
   - (B)   Obltn. Heinz Harry
           Scholz   (d) (Glogau, 10.1.1916)
   - (Bf) Uffz. Kurt Schraps   (u) (Zwönitz, 6.12.1918)
   - (Bm) Uffz. Günter Weidner   (d) (Solingen, 23.8.1915)
   - (Bs) Uffz. Josef Hanft   (d) (Hohn, 14.6.1915)

5. 1210 hrs. Westfield Farm, Studland, near Swanage, Dorset. Shot down by fighters.
   He 111 P (W.Nr.6305), G1+BH of 1./K.G.55
   - (F)   Fw. Fritz Jürges   (w)(Fürstenberg, 30.3.1915)

     (B)   Hptm. Karl Köthke   (u) (Harburg, 9.9.1906)
     (Bf) Gefr. Rudolf Weisbach (u) (Germersheim, 7.12.1919)
     (Bm) Uffz. Josef Altrichter (d) (Lindau, 10.11.1918)
     (Bs) Fl. Otto Müller   (w)(Dudweiler, 12.5.1922)

6. Caen, France. Damaged by fighters. Crash landed.
   He 111 P (W.Nr.1579), G1+AP of 6./K.G.55
      (B)   Obltn. Helmut Kindor (w)
      (Bs) Uffz. Erich Turek   (w)
   Remainder of crew unhurt.

7. Ditched in the English Channel. Damaged by fighters. Crew rescued by
   the German Air/Sea Rescue organisation (Seenotdienst).
   Bf 110 C (W.Nr.3263) of III./Z.G.26

8. Theville, France. Damaged by fighters (60% damaged in subsequent
   crash-landing). Crew unhurt.
   Bf 110 C4 (W.Nr.2194)

9. Damaged (20%) in crash landing in France (precise location not known)
   after fighter action. Crew unhurt.
   Bf 110 C4 (W.Nr.2130)

Note: Crash times and locations from British records. Remaining details taken from
German records. Crew category: (F) = Flugzeugfuhrer (pilot); (B) = Beobachter
(observer); Bf = Bordfunker (wireless operator); (Bm) = Bordmechaniker
(flight mechanic); (Bs) = Bordschütze (gunner). Fate of crew member: (u) =
unwounded; (w) = wounded or injured; (d) = dead; (m) = missing.
Place and date of birth given when known.

Appendix 7

No 238 Squadron (Hawker Hurricane Mk I)
(Blue Section only)

Plt Off J.R. Urwin-Mann	P4232
Sgt J. Jeka (Poland)	P3836

No 56 Squadron (Hawker Hurricane Mk I)

Sq Ldr H.M. Pinfold	P2910
Plt Off K.T. Marston +	P2866
Plt Off D.C. MacKenzie + (New Zealand)	P3514
Plt Off B.J. Wicks +	P3874
Plt Off Z. Nozowicz (Poland)	P3870
Flt Lt R.E.P. Brooker +	P3421
Sgt P. Hillwood	N2434
Flg Off M.H. Constable-Maxwell	–
Flt Lt A.S.J. Edwards (Ireland)	–
Sgt C. Whitehead +	–
Flg Off F.W. Higginson	–
Sgt G. Smythe	–

No 609 (West Riding) Squadron (Vickers Supermarine Spitfire Mk IA)

Flg Off J.C. Dundas +	X4472
Sgt J. Hughes-Rees +	L1096
Plt Off M.E. Staples +	X4234
Plt Off A.K. Ogilvie (Canada)	R6706
Plt Off R.F.G. Miller +(Australia)	X4107
Plt Off J.D. Bisdee	X4165
Sq Ldr H.S. Darley	P9503
Plt Off D.M. Crook +	R6961
Plt Off N. le C. Agazarian +	R6915 *
Flg Off T.H.T. Forshaw	X4471
Plt Off J. Curchin +	R6631
Flg Off T. Nowierski (Poland)	N3223

* This aircraft survived the war and is currently on display at the Imperial War Museum, London.

No 152 Squadron (Vickers Supermarine Spitfire Mk IA)

Flt Lt D.P.A. Boitel-Gill +	– Returned to base with engine trouble
Plt Off R.F. Inness	–
Plt Off C.S. Cox	–
Plt Off T.M. Bayles	–
Plt Off F.H. Holmes +	–
Plt Off R.M.D. Hall	–
Flt Lt F.M. Thomas	–
Plt Off A.R. Watson +	–
Plt Off D.W. Williams	–
Sgt H.J. Ackroyd +	–

No 504 (County of Nottingham) Squadron (Hawker Hurricane Mk I)

Flt Lt A.H. Rook	V6702
Sgt C. Haw	P3415
Plt Off E.M. Frisby +	P2987
Flg Off M.E.A. Royce	P3388
Sgt D. Haywood	N2481
Plt Off M. Rook +	P3614
Flt Lt W.B. Royce	V6731
Plt Off J.R. Hardacre +	P3414
Plt Off C.M. Stavert	V6695
Plt Off B.E. White +	L1583
Sgt H.D.B. Jones +	V6732
Sgt B.M. Bush	N2669

+ Killed In Action or On Active Service during the war.

Appendix 8

RAF COMBAT CLAIMS – DEFENCE OF YATE
27 September, 1940

Squadron	Destroyed	Probably Destroyed	Damaged
No 238	½ Bf 110 (shared)	–	1 Bf 110
No 56	1 Bf 110	–	2 Bf 110
	1 Do 17		1 Do 17
No 609	6 Bf 110	1 Bf 110	1 Bf 110
	1 Bf 109		
No 152	3 Bf 110	–	3 Bf 110
	1 Ju 88		
	1 Bf 109		
No 504	6 Bf 110	–	3 Bf 110
Totals:	20½	1	11

Note: The claims shown here are those recorded in the Squadron's Operations Record Books and are not verified. Aircraft other than Bf 110s and Bf 109s are wrongly identified as only German aircraft of these types were involved.

Appendix 9

RAF CASUALTIES – DEFENCE OF YATE
27 September, 1940

Aircraft type and Serial No.	Squadron	Pilot	Time and Place
Spitfire Mk.IA X4107 (Category 3)	609	Plt.Off. R.F.G. Miller (killed)	1145 hrs. Collision with Bf 110. Crashed at Chesilbourne, near Piddlehinton, Dorset.
Hurricane Mk.I P3415 (Category 2)	504	Sgt. C. Haw (unhurt)	Approximately 1215 hrs. Forced landed at Axminster, Somerset.

Note 1. Several Spitfires of No 152 Squadron were also very slightly damaged.
Note 2. See Footnote, Appendix 5, for definitions of Category 2 and 3 damage.

Appendix 10

GERMAN CASUALTIES – ATTACK ON YATE
27 September, 1940

1. 1145 hrs. Stapleton Institution, Fishponds, Bristol. Shot down by a Hurricane of No 504 Squadron.
   Bf 110 C4 (W.Nr.2162), U8+FK of 2./Z.G.26
   (F) Ofw. Hans Tiepelt   (d) (Schildberg, 6.11.1913)
   (Bf) Uffz. Herbert Brosig   (d) (Bochum, 1.12.1919)

2. 1145 hrs. Haydon Farm, near Radstock, Somerset. Shot down by a Hurricane of No 504 Squadron.
   Bf 110 C4 (W.Nr.3571), U8+CL of 3./Z.G.26
   (F) Ltn. Joachim Koepsell   (u) (Lübbecke, 1.5.1919)
   (Bf) Uffz. Johann Schmidt   (d) (Günnigfeld, 4.9.1919)

3. 1200 hrs. Bussey Stool Farm, Tarrant Gunville, Dorset. Shot down in fighter action.
   Bf 110 D3 (W.Nr.3378), S9+DH of Erpr.Gr.210
   (F) Hptm. Martin Lutz
         (Gr.Kdr.)   (d) (Mannheim, 10.3.1913)
   (Bf) Uffz. Anton Schön   (d) (Stennweiler, 22.5.1918)

4. 1145 hrs. Bellamy's Farm, near Piddletrenthide, Dorset. Collided with a Spitfire of No 609 Squadron.
   Bf 110 C4 (W.Nr.3297), 3U+FT of 9./Z.G.26
   (F) Gefr. Georg Jackstedt   (w)
   (Bf) Gefr. Emil Lidtke   (d)

5. 1200 hrs. The Beeches, near Iwerne Minster, Dorset. Shot down in fighter action.
   Bf 110 DO (W.Nr.4270), S9+DU of 2./Erpr.Gr.210
   (F) Fw. Friedrich Ebner   (w) (Tubingen, 21.6.1915)
   (Bf) Gefr. Werner Zwick   (w) (Pirmasens, 4.6.1920)

6. 1145 hrs. Salter's Wood, Middle Bere Farm, near Arne, Wareham, Dorset. Fighter action, totally destroyed.
   Bf 110 C7 (W.Nr.3629), 3U+IM of 4./Z.G.26
   (F) Obltn. Arthur Niebuhr   (d)
   (Bf) Obgefr. Klaus Deissen   (d)

7. 1150 hrs. 2 miles East of Kimmeridge, Dorset. Bf 110 shot down in fighter action; identification not certain, but believed to be as follows:—

Bf 110 C4 (W.Nr.2168), 3U+BD of Gruppenstab III./Z.G.26
(F) Obltn. Hans Barschel   (d)
(Bf) Uffz. Klose   (d)

8. 1145 hrs. 1 mile South-West of Kimmeridge, Dorset. Shot down in fighter action.
Bf 110 C4 (W.Nr.3290), 3U+DS of 8./Z.G.26
(F) Uffz. Fritz Schupp   (w)
(Bf) Gefr. Karl Nechwatal (w)

9. Approx. 1200 hrs. According to German reports crashed in sea off the Dorset coast during fighter action.
Bf 110 D3 (W.Nr.3888), S9+JH of 1./Erpr.Gr.210
(F) Ltn. Gerhard Schmidt (d) (Güstrow, 3.7.1918)
(Bf) Fw. Gerhard Richter   (d) (Magdeburg, 5.8.1915)

10. Approx. 1200 hrs. According to German reports crashed in sea off the Dorset coast during fighter action. Crew missing.
Bf 110 DO (W.Nr.2248), S9+GK of 2./Erpr.Gr.210
(F) Obltn. Wilhelm Rössiger
     (Staffelkapitän)   (m)(Hamburg, 12.12.1913)
(Bf) Ofw. Hans Marx   (m)(Hannover, 18.5.1912)

Note: For abbreviations see the Footnote to Appendix 6.

Appendix 11

British and German Aircraft – Specifications and Performance.*

Hawker Hurricane Mk I:
   Dimensions: Span, 40 ft 0 in; length, 31 ft 4 in; height, 12 ft 11½ in;
      wing area, 258 sq ft.
   Weights: Empty, 4,982 lb; normal loaded, 6,477 lb.
   Engine: One Rolls-Royce Merlin III, rated 880 hp for take-off, 990
      hp at 12,250 ft, and 1,030 hp at 16,250 ft.
   Armament: Eight 0·303 in Browning Mk II machine-guns with 334
      rpg.
   Performance: Initial climb rate, 2,300 ft/min; climb rate at 11,000 ft,
      2,420 ft/min; time to 15,000 ft, 6·5 min; time to 20,000 ft, 9·8
      min; service ceiling, 34,200 ft. Maximum speed, 254 mph at sea
      level, 324 mph at 15,650 ft. Cruising speed, 190 mph.

Supermarine Spitfire Mk IA:
   Dimensions: Span, 36 ft 10 in; length, 29 ft 11 in; height, 11 ft 5 in;
      wing area, 242 sq ft.
   Weights: Empty, 4,810 lb; normal loaded, 5,820 lb.
   Engine: One Rolls-Royce Merlin III, rated at 880 hp for take-off,
      990 hp at 12,250 ft, and 1,030 hp at 16,250 ft.
   Armament: Eight 0·303 in Browning Mk II machineguns with 330
      rpg.
   Performance: Maximum climb rate, 2,500 ft/min; time to 15,000 ft,
      6·2 min; time to 20,000 ft, 9·4 min; service ceiling, 34,000 ft.
      Maximum speed, 355 mph at 19,000 ft; cruising speed, 205 mph.

Messerschmitt Bf 109 E3:
   Dimensions: Span, 32 ft 4½ in; length, 28 ft 4½ in; height, 8 ft 2⅓ in;
      wing area, 176·53 sq ft.
   Weights: Empty, 4,685 lb; loaded, 5,875 lb.
   Engine: One Daimler-Benz DB 601 Aa, rated at 1,100 hp for take-off
      and 1,020 hp at 14,765 ft.
   Armament: Two 20 mm MG FF cannon with 60 rpg in wings and
      two 7·9 mm MG 17 machine-guns with 1,000 rpg. (Alternative
      armament two 7·9 mm MG 17 machine-guns with 500 rpg and
      one engine-mounted MG FF/M 20 mm cannon with 180
      rounds.)

Performance: Initial climb rate 3,280 ft/min; time to 9,840 ft, 3·1 min; time to 19,685 ft, 7·1 min; service ceiling, 34,450 ft. Maximum speed 348 mph at 14,560 ft; cruising speed 233 mph. Maximum range 410 miles.

Messerschmitt Bf 110 C4:

Dimensions: Span, 53 ft 4¾ in, length 39 ft 8½ in, height, 11 ft 6 in; wing area, 413 sq ft.

Weights: Empty, 11,466 lb; loaded, 14,844 lb.

Engines: Two Daimler-Benz DB 601 A1, each rated at 1,050 hp for take-off and 1,100 hp at 12,140 ft.

Armament: Two 20 mm MG FF cannon with 180 rpg and four 7·9 mm MG 17 machine-guns with 1,000 rpg firing forward and one rear mounted 7·9 mm MG 15 machine-gun with 750 rpg.

Performance: Initial climb rate, 2,165 ft/min. Time to 19,685 ft, 10·2 min; service ceiling, 32,810 ft. Maximum speed 336 mph at 19,685 ft; cruising speed, 217 mph. Range with normal internal fuel at maximum continuous cruise, 481 miles; economical cruise range, 680 miles at 13,780 ft.

Heinkel He 111 P2:

Dimensions: Span, 74 ft 1 ¾ in, length, 53 ft 9½ in, height, 13 ft 1½ in; wing area, 942 sq ft.

Weights: Empty equipped, 17,670 lb; maximum loaded, 29,762 lb.

Engines: Two Daimler-Benz DB 601 A1, each rated at 1,100 hp for take-off and 1,015 hp at 14,765 ft.

Armament: Defensive:- Six 7·9 mm MG 15 machine-guns.

Offensive:- Maximum bomb load, 4,408 lb.

Performance: Maximum speed at sea level, 176 mph; at 6,560 ft, (Max load) 190 mph; at 16,400 ft, 200 mph. Cruising speed at 85% power, 193 mph at 16,400 ft (max load). Maximum range, 1,224 miles at 9,840 ft. Time to 6,560 ft, 14·2 min at 29,762 lb. Service ceiling, 26,250 ft (14,765 ft at maximum loaded condition).

* These details relate to the variants most widely in service on 25th-27th September 1940 and used in the operations described in this book.

INDEX

INDEX

Abbots Leigh, 107
Acklington, 43
Ackroyd, Sgt H.J., 208
Agazarian, Plt Off Noel le C., 100, 143, 188, 202, 207
Aldershot, 55
Aldwinkle, Plt Off A.J.H., 99, 194, 202
Altrichter, Uffz Josef, 102, 137, 138, 206
Anderson, Sq Ldr M.F., 201
Andover, 39, 43, 70
Anti-aircraft guns, 40
Antrup, Obltn Wilhelm, 43, 196, 200
Arne, 191, 210
Attern, 61
Auxiliary Air Force, 40
Avonmouth, 70, 119
Axminster, 70, 183, 208

Ball, C.B., 116, 196
Balloon Centre, No 11 (Pucklechurch), 40
Balloon Command, 40
Balloon Command, No 32 Group, 40
Balloon Squadrons: No 927, 40; No 935, 40; No 951, 40
Barnes, Leslie, 117
Baron, Oberwerkmeister, 98
Barrage Balloons, 40
Barry, 39
Barschel, Obltn Hans, 191, 211
Bath, 39, 70, 94, 99
Batt, Sgt L.G., 202
Bayles, Plt Off T.N., 77, 78, 96, 184, 202, 208
Bayreuth, 56
Beaumont-le-Roger, 51
Beauvais, 32
Beaverbrook, Lord, 112, 146, 148
Beck, Gefr Rudolf, 205

Bf 109 E3, Messerschmitt, 212, 213
Bf 110 C4, Messerschmitt, 213
Bibury, 39, 43, 70, 201
Birmingham, 198
Bisdee, Plt Off John D., 188, 207
Blandford Forum, 70, 186
Bodemeyer, Hptm Otto, 200
Boelcke Geschwader, 60
Boitel-Gill, Flt Lt D.P.A., 74, 77, 100, 202, 208
Boltenstern, Hptm von, 157
Bombs, German, 59
Boscombe Down, 39, 44, 70, 97, 144, 165, 184, 201
Bourges, 57
Bournemouth, 39, 70, 100, 164
Box, Wilts, 37, 39, 84, 201
Boyton, 70, 99, 125, 205
Brand, AVM Sir Quintin, 40, 41, 201
Brandstätt, 62
Brandt, Hptm Helmut, 95, 103, 123, 124, 200, 205
Branksome Chine, Poole, 128
Branksome Park, Poole, 101, 128
Bremen, 137, 199
Bridewell, Bristol, 120, 121
Bristol, 25, 26, 30, 34, 37, 38, 39, 44, 52, 66, 70, 82, 88, 113, 119, 122, 145-148, 151, 153, 155, 158, 171, 173, 174, 179, 191, 204
Bristol Aeroplane Company, 25, 26, 30-33, 44, 107, 108, 122, 140, 151, 153, 188
  Aircraft: Beaufighter, 28, 111, 112; Beaufort, 28; Blenheim, 28, 29; Bombay, 27; Box Kite, 26; F2B, 26; Type 134, 28
  Engines: Hercules, 28; Mercury, 28; Pegasus, 28; Perseus, 28, 30; Taurus, 28
Bristol Channel, 39, 53, 70, 83, 84

British Aerospace, 28
British and Colonial Aeroplane Company, 26
Brittany, 51
Bröcker, Obltn Hans, 65, 80, 102, 128, 200, 205
Brooker, Flt Lt R.E.P., 207
Brookwood Military Cemetery, 187, 191
Brosig, Uffz Herbert, 170, 174, 210
Brussels, 196
Budde, Gefr Rudolf, 63
Bundeswehr, 197
Bush, Sgt B.M., 183, 208

Caen, 103, 206
Calais, 57
Calne, 70, 83
Candy, Wilfred J., 179, 180, 196
Cardiff, 39, 70, 82
Casimir, Hptm Artur von, 139
Cerne Abbas, 70, 183, 195
Chambers, Mr, 187, 188
Channel Islands, 51
Charlton, 155, 171
Charmy Down, 70, 99, 204
Chartres, 46, 48, 52, 58, 65
Château Monteclin, 46
Chater, Flt Lt H.A., 201
Chelvey, 107
Cherbourg, 50, 53, 55, 68, 71, 72, 156, 164, 176, 184
Chesilbourne, 188, 209
Christchurch, 70, 189
Cirencester, 39, 43, 70
Clevedon, 70, 117, 198
Clifton, Bristol, 37
Coldstream Guards, 178, 180
Colerne, 70
Compiègne, 57
Condor Legion, 190
Constable-Maxwell, Flg Off Michael H., 183, 184, 190, 207
Constantinople, 44
Cooke, Miss Dorothy, 117, 118
Cosmos Engineering Company, 26
Cox, Plt Off C.S., 77, 184, 202, 204, 208
Cranbourne Chase, 70, 190
Cranfield, 194
Crook, Plt Off David M.,188, 194, 207

Croydon, 156
Curchin, Plt Off J., 143, 202, 207

Dachau, 196
Darley, Sq Ldr Horace S. ('George'), 44, 74, 82, 144, 194, 201, 202, 207
Davis, Sgt, 118
Debden, 43
Deissen, Obgefr Klaus, 210
Denain/Valenciennes, 156
Detmold, 138
Devitt, Sq Ldr Peter K., 43, 94, 97, 201, 202, 204
Digby, 173
Dix, Sgt, 116
Dobrick, Hptm Walter, 200
Dorchester, 70
Dowding, ACM Sir Hugh, 40, 146, 148, 188
Dresden, Kriegsschule, 56, 66
Dreux, 46, 48
Dundas, Flg Off John C., 143, 188, 194, 202, 207
Dunkirk, 180, 199

East Yorks Regiment, 191
Eastleigh, 39, 70
Ebner, Fw Fritz, 190, 210
Edwards, Flt Lt A.S.J., 207
Egypt, 44
Engel, Fw Georg, 61, 68, 75, 83, 86, 87, 116, 198, 205
Erprobungsgruppe 210, 34, 35, 72, 155-158, 164, 171, 176, 183, 184, 189-191, 196
Evreux, 55, 65
Exeter, 39, 43, 70-72, 76, 146, 201

Failand, 70, 107, 117, 123, 205
Fairey Aviation Works, 55
Feary, Sgt Alan N., 143, 202
Feltham, 55, 65
Fenton, Sq Ldr Harold A., 89, 94, 143, 201, 203
Fernaufklärungsgruppe 121, 34
Fernaufklärungsgruppe 123, 34, 149
Fighter aircraft:
    Gloster Gladiator, 40
    Hawker Hurricane Mk I, 40, 41, 212

Vickers Supermarine Spitfire Mk IA, 40, 41, 212

Messerschmitt Bf 109 E, 51, 212, 213

Messerschmitt Bf 110 C, 48, 50, 213

Fighter Command, 30, 40, 146

Fighter Command, No 10 Group, 30, 39, 40, 71, 72, 111, 146, 147, 201

Fighter Command, No 11 Group, 147

Fighter Command Squadrons:
No 56, 39, 44, 97, 144, 164, 166, 183, 184, 190, 195

No 79, 39, 81, 144

No 87, 39, 43

No 137, 195

No 152, 39, 43, 71, 72, 74, 82, 94, 100, 164, 184, 190, 195

No 234, 41

No 238, 39, 43, 89, 99, 101, 143, 164, 184, 195

No 247, 41

No 504, 148, 149, 166-169, 183, 185, 189, 190, 195

No 601, 39, 43, 72

No 609, 39, 44, 71, 72, 82, 100, 143, 164, 184, 188, 189

No 611, 195

Filton, 25-30, 32, 36, 38, 39, 41, 43, 47, 52-58, 65, 67, 73, 81, 84, 89, 90, 92, 105-113, 138, 145, 148, 153-157, 166, 168, 171, 173, 175, 183, 185, 189, 196, 198

Filton Sector Station, 37

Filton, Target Documents, 31, 32, 33, 35, 140

Fischerhude, 137

Fishponds, Bristol, 70, 172, 174, 190, 210

Flax Bourton, 70, 87, 117-119

Fliegerdivision 5, 56

Fliegerkorps V, 50, 196

Fonthill Bishop, 127

Forshaw, Flg Off T.H.T., 188, 202, 207

Frazer Nash, Capt A.G., 158, 162

Frisby, Plt Off E. Murray, 153, 154, 169, 170, 171, 175, 190, 195, 208

Frome, 70, 99, 164, 180, 204

Führungsstab, 32

Gabriel, Hptm Hans-Joachim, 56, 60, 200

Geib, Gefr Karl, 61, 75, 86, 87, 117, 118, 121, 198, 205

Gerdsmeier, Uffz Karl, 52-57, 60, 61, 75, 83, 84, 86, 87, 115, 116, 118, 120, 198, 205

German aircraft: Bf 109, 51, 212, 213; Bf 110, 48, 50, 213; Do 17, 82, 143; Do 215, 82, 143; He 111, 32, 47, 48, 213; Ju 88, 34, 57; Me 210, 156

Giessen, 45

Glastonbury, 70, 82, 204

Gonne, Major, 119

Göring, Reichsmarschall Hermann, 45

Grater, Kenneth, 85, 195

Gratton-Thompson, Capt E., 159

Greenbank Cemetery, Bristol, 174

Greim, Generalmajor Ritter von, 56

Guderian's Panzerkorps, 56

Guernsey, 51

Hall, Plt Off R.M.D., 185, 186, 202, 208

Ham Green Hospital, Bristol, 38

Hanft, Uffz Josef, 131, 132, 205

Hardacre, Plt Off J.R., 208

Harms, Obltn Otto-Bernhard, 200

Harrison, Plt Off D.S., 99, 203, 204

Harrison, V.C., 121

Haw, Sgt Charlton 'Wag', 183, 185, 195, 208, 209

Haywood, Sgt D., 185, 208

Heathrow, 55, 65

He 111 P2, Heinkel, 213

Hendon, 43, 44, 148, 149

Hendy Aircraft Company, 158

Hendy aircraft: Elf, 159; Heck, 159; Imp, 159; Pixie, 159

Herbst, Fw August, 110

Heyworth, Sq Ldr J.E., 201

Higginson, Plt Off F.W., 184, 207

Hillwood, Sgt P, 207

Hind, Hawker, 167

Hitler, Adolf, 57

Höfer, Hptm Heinz, 198, 200

Holder, Hubert 87

Holland, Sgt Kenneth C, 97, 195, 202, 204

Holmes, Plt Off F.H., 77, 184, 195, 202, 208
Holton Heath, 39
Hope, Sq Ldr Sir Archibald P., 43, 201
Horsky, Sgt V., 203
Horsley, Hawker, 167
Hughes Rees, Sgt J., 82, 143, 202, 204, 207
Hurricane, Hawker, 40, 41, 212
Huth, Obstltn Joachim-Friedrich, 49, 50, 157
Hyde Park, 139

Illesheim, 62
Imperial War Museum, 188, 197, 207
Inness, Plt Off R.F., 74, 77, 184, 202, 208
Isle of Wight, 39, 70, 72, 186, 194, 195
Iwerne Minster, 70, 190, 210

Jackstedt, Gefr Georg, 186, 187, 210
Jafu 2, 50
Jafu 3, 50
Jagdgeschwader 2, 34, 45, 51, 163, 164, 189
Jagdgeschwader 53, 34, 45, 51, 163, 189
Jankiewicz, Flg Off J.S., 99, 202
Janku, Mr and Mrs Theo, 133, 134, 196
Jefferies, Mrs 154
Jeka, Sgt, 184, 207
Jesuiter, Ofw, 81
Jones, Glyn, 107
Jones, Sgt H.B.D., 168, 175, 179, 185, 208
Jürges, Fw Fritz, 95, 102, 133, 138, 139, 199, 205

Kampfgeschwader 27, 34
Kampfgeschwader 51, 45, 72
Kampfgeschwader 54, 45, 72
Kampfgeschwader 55, 32, 45-48, 53, 55-57, 60, 62, 63, 66, 89, 196, 198
Kampfgeschwader 77, 57
Kampfgeschwader 154, 45
Kampfgeschwader 155, 45
Kampfgeschwader 254, 45
Karbe, Obltn Adalbert, 200
Keating, Colonel, 135

Kenley, 156
Kiel/Holtenau, 62
Kiel, Hptm Rudolf, 95, 200
Kimmeridge, 70, 191, 210, 211
Kindor, Obltn Helmut, 97, 103, 199, 206
Kings, Plt Off A.R., 143, 203
King's Cup Air Races, 159
Kirchoff, Ofw Rudolf, 205
Kless, Maj Friedrich, 48, 52, 56, 57, 81, 84, 88, 89, 105, 196, 200
Kless, Maj Max, 57
Klose, Uffz, 191, 211
Klotzsche Luftkriegsschule, 63
Koepsell, Ltn Joachim, 174, 176-180, 182, 195, 199, 210
Königsberg, 188
Korte, Obstltn Hans, 46, 57, 66, 200
Köthke, Hptm Karl, 95, 102, 103, 136-138, 199, 206
Krakau, 63
Krazer, Hptm Dr Karl, 200
Kucera, Sgt J., 203
Kühl, Maj Dr Ernst, 46, 197, 200

La Boissière-le-Déluge, 32
Langendiebach, 45, 139
Langsdorff, Hptm Hans Otto von, 200
Le Havre, 50, 156
Lidtke, Gefr Emil, 186, 187, 210
Little, Sgt R., 96, 203
London, 26, 56, 57, 133
Lublin, 196
Ludwigsburg, 199
Luftflotte 3, 32, 107
Luftflottenkommando Ost, 196
Luftflottenkommando 6, 196
Lufttransportführer Stalingrad, 197
Luftwaffe, 51
Luftwaffe High Command Operations Staff, 32
Luftwaffe 5 Abteilung, 28, 31, 162
Lulworth Cove, 70, 74
Lutz, Hptm Martin, 157, 164, 169, 190, 192, 210
Lyme Bay, 70, 74

Machold, Ofw Werner, 51, 189
MacKenzie, Plt Off D.C., 184, 207
Makrocki, Hptm Wilhelm, 49, 50

Malta, 195
Manor Park Hospital, Bristol, 173
Marrs, Plt Off Eric S., 78-80, 195, 202, 204
Marshallsay, Mrs, 133, 136, 138, 196
Marston, Plt Off K.T., 184, 207
Marx, Ofw Hans, 192, 211
Matthews, Leslie and Gladys, 123
Mayers, Flg Off H.C., 81, 99, 194, 202
McArthur, Flt Lt J.H.G., 143, 202
McBean Christie, Sgt J., 77, 195, 202
Meadway, Thomas, 96, 123, 124, 195
Mells, 70, 181
Mertz, Uffz Hans-Fritz, 205
Middle East, 194, 195
Middle Wallop, 39, 43, 44, 70, 72, 76, 99, 103, 146, 164, 184, 201
Miller, Plt Off R.F.G, 100, 143, 164, 186-189, 202, 207, 209
Mills, Sq Ldr R.S., 201
Morane Saulnier MS 406, 61
Müller, Fl Otto, 138, 139, 199, 206

Nailsea, 107
Narres, Ofw Alfred, 61, 76, 84, 86, 118, 198, 205
Nash and Thompson, Ltd, 158, 162
Nechwatel, Gefr Karl, 191, 211
Needles, The, 70, 74
Netheravon, 70
Neudorf/Opeln, 46
Newbury, Flg Off J.C., 202
Newport, 39
Newton St Loe, 70, 94, 204
Niebuhr, Obltn Arthur, 210
Normandy, 53
Northolt, 44, 188
Norway, 48
Nowierski, Flg Off T., 143, 202, 207
Nozowicz, Plt Off Z., 207

Oberkommando der Luftwaffe, 32
Oberländer, Obltn Werner, 65, 66, 103, 104, 198
O'Brien, Sq Ldr J.S., 201
Observer Corps, (No 23 Group), 37, 39
Ogilvie, Plt Off A. Keith, 143, 194, 202. 207

Oiseme, 58
Oldham, 121, 127, 133, 140
Old Sarum, 70
Ostaszewski, Flg Off, 202
Ostend, 62
Oxford, 136

Paris, 32, 57
Parnall Aircraft Company, 155, 158, 159, 162
    Target Documents, 160-163
Parnall, George, 158
Parow, Seefliegerschule, 62
Patchway, 29, 30, 108, 112, 155
Peacock, Mrs Alice, 109
Pembrey, 39, 43, 70, 77, 81, 144, 146, 201
Phipps, Mr S., 37, 38
Piddlehinton, 187, 209
Piddletrenthide, 70, 187, 190, 210
Pill, Bristol, 38
Pinfold, Sq Ldr Harold M., 44, 164, 201, 207
Poland, 26, 48
Poole, 39, 70, 100, 101, 128-130, 133, 183, 186, 189, 190, 205
Porlock Weir, 70
Portbury, 85-87
Portishead, 38, 70, 82, 85
Portland, 39, 55, 72, 74, 75, 100, 155, 164, 188
Portland Bill, 53, 70, 71, 72, 74, 76, 188, 191
Port Talbot, 39

Radstock, 70, 99, 166, 179-181, 190, 195, 199, 204, 210
Regional Commissioner, South West Region, 192
Reiser, Fw Martin L., 62, 63, 65, 104, 198
Rettburg, Hptm Ralph von, 49, 50
Richards, Sgt Major A.H., 119, 195
Richards, Capt, 119
Richter, Fw Gerhard, 191, 211
Roborough, 201
Rodney Works, 28, 107, 108, 112
Roeber, Hptm Joachim, 200
Rolls Royce, Ltd, 28, 53
Rook, Flt Lt Anthony H., 168, 175, 183, 190, 208

Rook, Flg Off Michael, 154, 173, 175, 183, 195, 208
Rössiger, Obltn Wilhelm, 164, 190-192, 211
Rouen, 57
Royal Artillery, 76th HAA Regiment, 37, 81, 85, 195
Royal Artillery, 73 LAA Battery, 38
Royce, Flg Off Michael E.A., 173, 195, 208
Royce, Flt Lt W Barrington, 152-154, 166-168, 170, 195, 208
Rozycki, Flg Off W., 143, 203
Rubensdörffer, Hptm Walter, 156, 157
Rudloe Manor, Box, 37, 201
Russia, 195

Saarbrücken, 199
Saint-Cloud, 32
Salisbury, 39, 70, 128
Sample, Sq Ldr John, 155, 166, 195
Scapa Flow, 148
Schalk, Hptm Hans, 49, 50
Schemmell, Maj Hans, 47, 200
Scherer, Frau Grete, 198
Scherer, Fw Walter, 97-99, 125-128, 198, 205
Schirmböck, Obltn Josef, 200
Schmidt, Ltn Gerhard, 191, 211
Schmidt, Uffz Johann, 176, 177, 180, 210
Schmidtke, Erich, 55
Scholz, Obltn Heinz, 128, 131, 205
Schön, Uffz Anton, 190, 210
Schraps, Uffz Kurt, 128, 129, 131-133, 199, 205
Schumacher, Gefr Heinz, 97, 128, 205
Schupp, Uffz Fritz, 191, 211
Sedan, 57
Shaftesbury, 70, 127, 164, 190
Sheppard, Mr, 130
Shepton Mallett, 70
Shirehampton, Bristol, 118, 119
Shroton, 190
Sibley, Sgt F.A., 99, 203, 204
Simmonds, Plt Off Vernon C., 143, 203
Sinclair, Sir Archibald, 188
Smith, John, 117
Smythe, Sgt G., 207

Somerset Ashcott, 107
Southampton, 39, 70, 186, 196
Southmead, Bristol, 108
Spencer, Sgt, 185
Sperrle, Generalfeldmarschall Hugo, 32
Spitfire Mk IA, Vickers Supermarine, 40, 41, 212
St Albans Head, 164
St Eval, 39, 41, 201
Standford, 107
Staples, Plt Off M.E., 143, 188, 202, 207
Stapleton Institution, Bristol, 173
Stavert, Plt Off C.M., 208
Sternberg, Obltn Johannes Speck von, 61, 63, 198, 200
Stöckl, Oberst Alois, 47
Stoke Gifford, 108
Stoke-under-Ham, 107
Studland, 70, 103, 133, 138, 143, 199, 205
Sturminster Newton, 70, 97
Suffolk Regiment, 135
Swanage, 70-72, 74, 76, 100, 133, 135, 205
Swansea, 39, 70
Sweet, Mr and Mrs, 180, 196
Swindon, 121

Tangmere, 43
Tarrant Gunville, 210
Taylor, John, 125
Territorial Army, 66th (South Midlands) Field Brigade, 37
Theville, 105, 206
Thiberville, 50
Thomas, Flt Lt F.M., 186, 208
Tiepelt, Ofw Hans, 170, 174, 210
Tongue, Plt Off Reginald E., 175
Tory, Philip, 187, 196
Tranter, Mrs Annie, 88
Trew, L.W., 128, 196
Tüffers, Ltn Adalbert, 63, 65
Turek, Uffz Erich, 206
Tyntesfield, 107

Upavon, 70
Urwin-Mann, Plt Off Jack R., 101, 143, 184, 195, 203, 207

Valentine, Dr G.A., 118
Versailles, 46
Villacoublay, 46, 52, 58, 63-65, 67, 104

Wallace, Westland, 167
Wareham, 70, 138, 191, 210
Warminster, 70, 127, 128
Warmwell, 39, 43, 70, 71, 74, 76, 77, 103, 164, 184, 201, 204
Warner, J.P.H., 134
Watson, Plt Off A.R., 186, 190, 208
Weidner, Uffz Günter, 131, 132, 205
Weigel, Obltn Gottfried, 60, 61, 65, 75, 76, 84, 87, 118-120, 199, 205
Weisbach, Gefr Rudolf, 137, 138, 199, 206
Well Bottom, 99
Westbury-on-Trym, 108
Westland Aircraft Company, 76
Weston Airport, 183
Weston-super-Mare, 53, 77, 81, 82, 84, 99
Weston Zoyland, 70
Weymouth, 39, 70, 71, 188
Wheeler, E., 130
Whirlwind, Westland, 195
Whitchurch, Bristol, 70
White, Plt Off B.E.G., 171, 208
White, Sir George, 26
White, Sir Stanley, 188
Whitehead, Sgt C., 207

Whitley, Armstrong-Whitworth, 162
Wick, Maj Helmut, 51, 189, 194
Wicks, Plt Off B.J., 207
Wigglesworth, Plt Off J.S., 103, 143, 203
Wightman, Ralph, 187, 196
Williams, Plt Off Dudley W., 95, 97, 99, 186, 202, 208
Wingrove, Douglas, 83, 195
Winterbourne, 108
Wittkamp, Ofw Günter, 205
Wittmer, Hptm Heinrich, 200
Wolton, Sgt R., 77, 202
Woolston, 70, 105, 149, 192, 196
Woolverton, 70, 97, 123, 195, 204, 205
Woolwich, 139, 198
Worth, 39

Yate, 70, 155, 156, 158, 159, 164, 179, 189, 210
Yatesbury, 70, 83, 148, 195
Yatton, 107
Yeovil, 39, 70, 76, 77, 81, 143, 146, 184
Yeovilton, 70

Zerstörergeschwader 26, 34, 45, 48, 50, 164, 174, 183, 189, 190, 191, 196
Zerstörergeschwader 1, 190
Zwick, Gefr Werner, 190, 210